TRIVQUIZ

1001

TRIVIA QUESTIONS

NEWCASTLE UNITED

FASCINATING FACTS! TRIVIA BRAINTEASERS!
WRITTEN AND ILLUSTRATED BY

Steve McGarry

DESIGNED BY JOE McGARRY

First published by Pitch Publishing, 2022

Pitch Publishing
A2 Yeoman Gate
Yeoman Way
Worthing
Sussex
BN13 3QZ
www.pitchpublishing.co.uk
info@pitchpublishing.co.uk

A CIP catalogue record is available for this book
from the British Library.

ISBN: 978 1 80150 016 6

Typesetting and origination by Pitch Publishing
Printed and bound in India by Replika Press Pvt. Ltd.

1001 TRIVIA QUESTIONS: NEWCASTLE UNITED

Other books in this series:

1001 TRIVIA QUESTIONS: ARSENAL
1001 TRIVIA QUESTIONS: MANCHESTER CITY
1001 TRIVIA QUESTIONS: MANCHESTER UNITED
1001 TRIVIA QUESTIONS: TOTTENHAM HOTSPUR
1001 TRIVIA QUESTIONS: WEST HAM UNITED
1001 TRIVIA QUESTIONS: THIS DAY IN WORLD FOOTBALL

ACKNOWLEDGEMENTS

Thanks to Joe McGarry for his brilliant design work and his technical expertise. There would be no books without him!

Thanks to Debs McGarry for the research and art assistance.

Thanks to Luke McGarry for picking up the slack on the other features while we worked on this.

Thanks to all three for their patience!

Additional thanks to Tom and Andy at "Shoot! The Breeze" podcast and Rob Stokes for the additional research and scans!

ABOUT STEVE McGARRY

A former record sleeve designer, whose clients included Joy Division, Steve McGarry is one of the most prolific and widely-published cartoonists and illustrators that Britain has ever produced. In the UK alone, his national newspaper daily strips include "Badlands", which ran for a dozen years in The Sun, "The Diary of Rock & Pop" in the Daily Star, "Pop Culture" in Today and "World Soccer Diary" in The Sun.

Over his four-decade career he has regularly graced the pages of soccer magazines Match, Match of the Day and Shoot! and his comics work ranges from Romeo in the 1970s and Look-In, Tiger and Oink! in the 1980s, SI for Kids and FHM in the 1990s, through to the likes of Viz, MAD and Toxic! When The People launched his Steve McGarry's 20th Century Heroes series, they billed him as the world's top cartoonist.

His sports features have been published worldwide since 1982 and he currently has two features – "Biographic" and "Kid Town" – in newspaper syndication, with a client list that includes the New York Daily News and The Washington Post.

In recent years, he has also created story art for such movies as "Despicable Me 2", "The Minions" and "The Secret Life of Pets".

Although Manchester born and bred, Steve has been based in California since 1989. A two-term former President of the National Cartoonists Society, his honours include Illustrator of the Year awards from the NCS and the Australian Cartoonists Association, and he is a recipient of the prestigious Silver T-Square for "outstanding service to the profession of cartooning". In 2013, he was elected President of the NCS Foundation, the charitable arm of the National Cartoonists Society. He is also the founder and director of US comics festival NCSFest.

1001 QUESTIONS

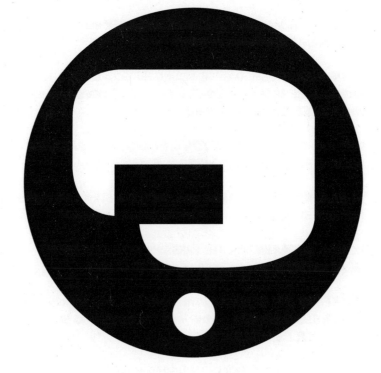

THE GALLOWGATE GIANT

BORN IN NEWCASTLE IN 1970, **ALAN SHEARER** WAS 17 YEARS AND 240 DAYS OLD WHEN TWO WEEKS AFTER MAKING HIS FULL DEBUT FOR **SOUTHAMPTON** HE BECAME THE YOUNGEST PLAYER TO SCORE AN ENGLISH TOP-FLIGHT HAT-TRICK. HE JOINED **BLACKBURN ROVERS** IN 1992, WHERE HE WON A PREMIER LEAGUE TITLE, BEFORE SIGNING FOR **NEWCASTLE UNITED** IN A WORLD RECORD £15 MILLION TRANSFER IN THE SUMMER OF 1996.

1 WHO WAS THE MANAGER WHO GAVE **SHEARER** HIS **SOUTHAMPTON** DEBUT IN 1988?

2 WHEN **SHEARER** BECAME THE YOUNGEST SCORER OF A TOP-FLIGHT HAT-TRICK, HE BROKE A RECORD SET THREE DECADES EARLIER BY WHICH **CHELSEA** GOALGETTER?

3 WHO WAS THE **SOUTHAMPTON** MANAGER WHEN **SHEARER** WAS SOLD TO **BLACKBURN ROVERS** IN 1992?

4 AT **BLACKBURN**, **SHEARER** WAS PART OF A STRIKE PARTNERSHIP, NICKNAMED "**THE SAS**", WITH WHICH OTHER FORWARD?

5 HOW DID **SHEARER** TELL THE PRESS HE WOULD CELEBRATE **BLACKBURN'S** 1995 PREMIER LEAGUE TITLE WIN?

6 **SIR KENNY DALGLISH** WAS THE MANAGER WHO SIGNED HIM TO **BLACKBURN ROVERS** -- WHO WAS THE BOSS WHO SOLD HIM TO **NEWCASTLE UNITED** IN 1996?

7 HE WAS RED-CARDED TWICE DURING HIS **NEWCASTLE** PLAYING DAYS -- NAME ONE OF THE OPPOSING TEAMS.

8 AFTER A DECADE ON TYNESIDE, HIS 2006 TESTIMONIAL GAME FEATURED **NEWCASTLE** AGAINST WHICH OPPONENTS?

9 IN 2021, **SHEARER** WAS AN INAUGURAL INDUCTEE INTO THE PREMIER LEAGUE HALL OF FAME. HOW MANY OF THE SEVEN OTHER INAUGURAL INDUCTEES CAN YOU NAME?

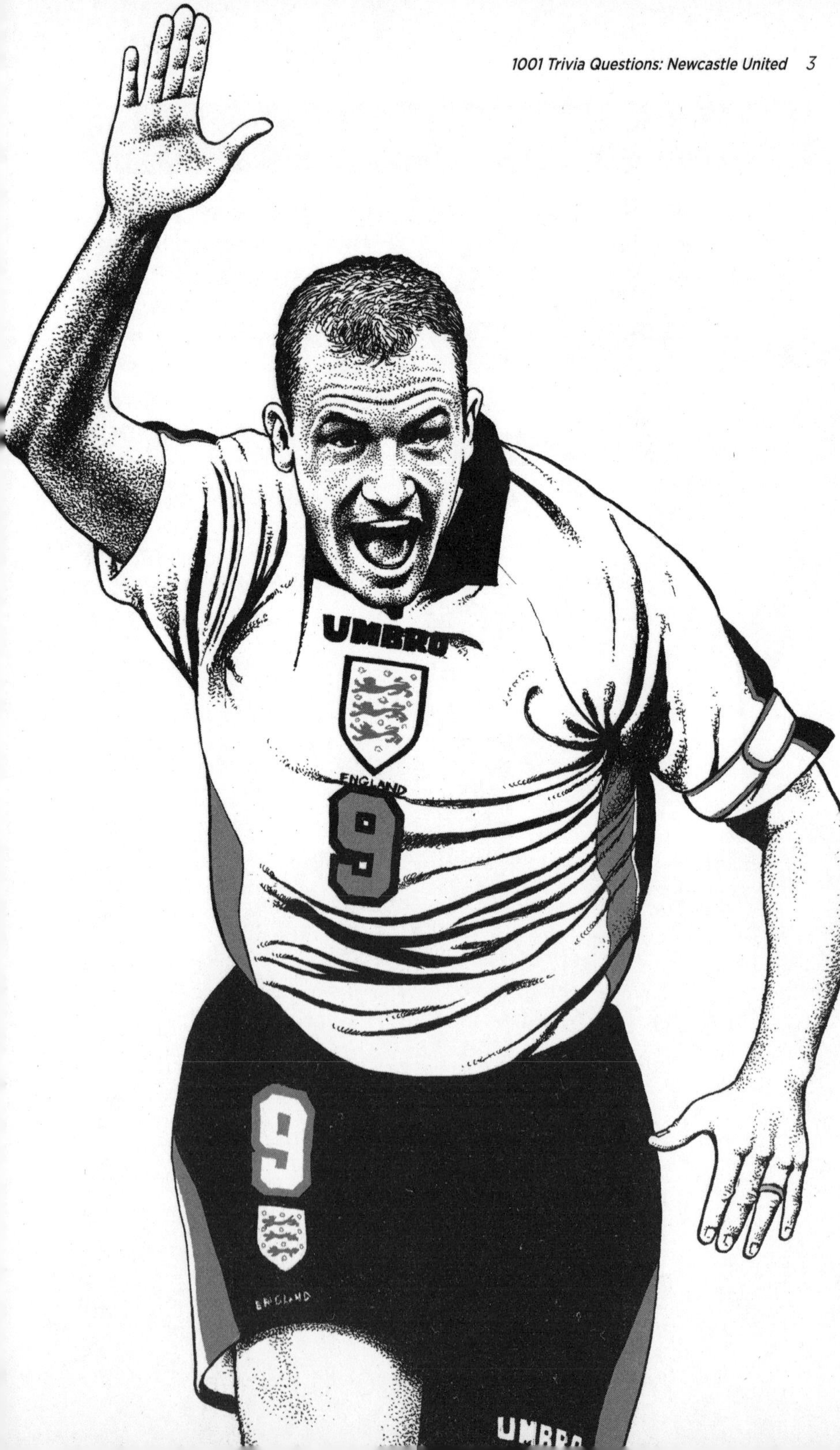
UMBRO
ENGLAND
9
9
ENGLAND
UMBRO

KING KEV

THE SON OF A **NEWCASTLE UNITED** SUPPORTER WHO WORKED IN A DONCASTER COLLIERY, **KEVIN KEEGAN** CAPTAINED **ENGLAND**, WON A EUROPEAN CUP AND WAS TWICE VOTED EUROPEAN FOOTBALL OF THE YEAR BEFORE HE BECAME A TYNESIDE LEGEND AS BOTH A PLAYER AND LATER MANAGER OF **NEWCASTLE**. SADLY, HIS GEORDIE DAD DIDN'T LIVE LONG ENOUGH TO SEE **"KING KEV"** PLAY FOR **NEWCASTLE**.

1 KEEGAN BEGAN HIS PROFESSIONAL CAREER AT WHICH CLUB?

2 WHICH MANAGER SIGNED KEEGAN TO LIVERPOOL IN 1971?

3 KEEGAN SCORED TWICE IN LIVERPOOL'S 3-0 FA CUP FINAL WIN OVER NEWCASTLE UNITED IN 1974, THE FIRST PLAYER TO SCORE TWICE IN THE FINAL SINCE MIKE TREBILCOCK SCORED A BRACE FOR WHICH TEAM IN 1966?

4 LATER THAT YEAR, DISMISSED FOR TRADING PUNCHES ON THE PITCH, KEEGAN AND WHICH OTHER PLAYER BECAME THE FIRST PLAYERS EVER DISMISSED IN A CHARITY SHIELD SEASON OPENER?

5 WHO WAS KEEGAN'S REPLACEMENT AT LIVERPOOL, A £440,000 SIGNING FROM CELTIC?

6 HE JOINED WHICH GERMAN TEAM IN A RECORD TRANSFER IN 1977, HELPING THE CLUB WIN A FIRST BUNDESLIGA TITLE IN 19 YEARS?

7 WHO WAS THE MANAGER WHO SIGNED KEVIN KEEGAN TO SOUTHAMPTON IN 1980?

8 WHO WAS THE MANAGER WHO SIGNED KEEGAN TO NEWCASTLE UNITED TWO YEARS LATER?

9 KEEGAN'S FINAL APPEARANCE FOR NEWCASTLE CAME IN A FRIENDLY AGAINST WHICH TEAM, AFTER WHICH HE LEFT THE PITCH IN A HELICOPTER WHILE STILL DRESSED IN HIS KIT?

10 HE BRIEFLY CAME OUT OF RETIREMENT TO PLAY TWO GAMES FOR BLACKTOWN CITY ... A TEAM BASED IN WHICH COUNTRY?

HOWAY THE YOUNG LADS!

BORN IN GATESHEAD ON MAY 27, 1967, *PAUL GASCOIGNE* WAS SIGNED BY *NEWCASTLE* AS A SCHOOLBOY IN 1980. HE SIGNED ON AS AN APPRENTICE ON HIS 16TH BIRTHDAY IN 1983 AND CAPTAINED THE YOUTH TEAM TO THE FA YOUTH CUP FINAL IN THE 1984-85 SEASON, SCORING TWICE IN THE 4-1 SECOND LEG VICTORY AWAY TO *WATFORD* AFTER A 0-0 DRAW IN THE FIRST LEG.

IT WAS THE SECOND TIME *"THE MAGPIES"* HAD WON THE COMPETITION, FOLLOWING THE 2-1 WIN OVER *WOLVES* IN THE 1962 FINAL. NAME THESE OTHER MEMBERS OF THOSE TWO TRIUMPHANT TEAMS WHO WENT ON TO CARVE OUT PROFESSIONAL CAREERS:

1 1962: HE WENT ON TO CAPTAIN **NEWCASTLE** AND **SCOTLAND**, SCORING THREE GOALS ACROSS TWO LEGS WHEN **NEWCASTLE** WON THE INTER-CITIES FAIRS CUP IN 1969. HE LATER PLAYED FOR **SUNDERLAND** AND **CARLISLE UNITED** AND MANAGED **CARLISLE, HEART OF MIDLOTHIAN, PLYMOUTH ARGYLE** AND **HARTLEPOOL UNITED.**

2 1985: STRIKER WHO WON PROMOTIONS WITH THREE DIFFERENT CLUBS, HE PLAYED FOR **CHELSEA, SWANSEA CITY** AND **BRENTFORD** AMONG OTHERS, AND IN THE FIRST OF HIS TWO SPELLS WITH **HARTLEPOOL UNITED**, HE SET THE CLUB RECORD OF 28 GOALS IN A SINGLE SEASON.

3 1985: SON OF A FAMED **REPUBLIC OF IRELAND** GOALKEEPER, HE MADE MORE THAN 50 APPEARANCES FOR **NEWCASTLE** BEFORE SPENDING SEVEN YEARS WITH **BURY** AND SEVEN WITH **OLDHAM ATHLETIC**, WINNING PLAYER OF THE YEAR AWARDS AT BOTH.

4 1962: RIGHT-BACK WHO WENT ON TO MAKE 460 APPEARANCES FOR THE CLUB, WINNING THE 1969 INTER-CITIES FAIRS CUP.

5 1985: DEFENDER WHO CAPTAINED **NEWCASTLE** TO THE FIRST DIVISION TITLE IN 1993, AFTER A DECADE AT THE CLUB HE JOINED **TOTTENHAM HOTSPUR** IN 1994.

6 1962: HE JOINED **BRIGHTON & HOVE ALBION** IN 1963, GOING ON TO CAPTAIN THE CLUB AND MAKE 338 APPEARANCES BEFORE SPENDING TWO SEASONS WITH **BLACKBURN ROVERS.**

7 1985: HAVING ESTABLISHED HIMSELF IN THE **NEWCASTLE** FIRST TEAM, HE JOINED **BRADFORD CITY** IN 1989, MOVING ON TO **BRISTOL CITY** FOUR YEARS LATER. HE WENT ON TO MAKE MORE THAN 450 APPEARANCES FOR THE CLUB, INCLUDING A SPELL AS PLAYER/MANAGER.

8 1962: MIDFIELDER WHO JOINED **BLACKPOOL** IN 1966 HAVING SCORED 43 GOALS IN 152 GAMES FOR *"THE MAGPIES"*. DURING HIS DECADE WITH THE CLUB HE WAS DUBBED "*THE KING OF BLOOMFIELD ROAD*" AND WAS AN INAUGURAL INDUCTEE TO **BLACKPOOL'S** HALL OF FAME.

THEY CROSSED THE TYNE-WEAR DIVIDE

SUNDERLAND-BORN **ALAN KENNEDY** PLAYED IN THE **NEWCASTLE** TEAM THAT LOST THE 1974 FA CUP FINAL TO **LIVERPOOL**, THE CLUB HE JOINED FOUR YEARS LATER. AFTER WINNING A PLETHORA OF HONOURS WITH THE MERSEYSIDERS, HE SIGNED FOR **SUNDERLAND** IN 1986.

IDENTIFY THESE OTHERS WHO PLAYED FOR BOTH **NEWCASTLE UNITED** AND **SUNDERLAND**:

1 THE FIRST PLAYER SINCE **LIONEL PÉREZ** IN 1998 TO TRANSFER DIRECTLY FROM **SUNDERLAND** TO **NEWCASTLE**, HIS 2014 MOVE CAUSED OUTRAGE AMONG *"THE MACKEMS"*, HE JOINED **NOTTINGHAM FOREST** ON A FREE TRANSFER IN 2020.

2 HAVING WON PROMOTION WITH **NEWCASTLE** IN 1993, HIS TIME WITH **SUNDERLAND** ENDED WHEN HE WAS SEEN WEARING A T-SHIRT WITH A DEROGATORY MESSAGE TO **"BLACK CATS"** FANS. HE WAS MOVED ON TO **FULHAM** AND LATER ENDED HIS PLAYING DAYS BACK ON TYNESIDE, BEFORE EMBARKING ON A MANAGEMENT CAREER THAT HAS SEEN HIM TAKE CHARGE OF A NUMBER OF CLUBS, INCLUDING **HUDDERSFIELD TOWN**, **BIRMINGHAM CITY**, **BLACKPOOL**, **KILMARNOCK**, **BURY** AND **BLYTH SPARTANS**.

3 **ENGLAND** INTERNATIONAL MIDFIELDER WHO HAD THREE SPELLS AT **SUNDERLAND**, THREE SEASONS AT **NEWCASTLE** AND WAS A 1985 EUROPEAN CUP WINNERS' CUP WINNER WITH **EVERTON**.

4 **FRANCE** INTERNATIONAL STRIKER WHO SPENT TIME ON LOAN AT **NEWCASTLE** IN 1999, BEFORE HIS CAREER TOOK HIM TO **FULHAM**, **MANCHESTER UNITED**, **EVERTON**, **TOTTENHAM HOTSPUR**, **SUNDERLAND** AND **LAZIO**.

5 **SUNDERLAND'S** CAPTAIN IN THE 1985 LEAGUE CUP FINAL, HE WON HONOURS WITH **LIVERPOOL** BEFORE JOINING **NEWCASTLE** IN 1992, HELPING **KEVIN KEEGAN'S** TEAM WIN PROMOTION. HE LATER PLAYED FOR **GALATASARAY** AND **SOUTHAMPTON**.

6 AFTER HIS RELATIONS WITH THE **NEWCASTLE** BOARD SOURED FOLLOWING HIS MOVE FROM **BRADFORD PARK AVENUE**, THE MAVERICK **ENGLAND** FORWARD JOINED **SUNDERLAND** FOR A BRITISH TRANSFER FEE RECORD OF £20,050 IN 1948.

7 **ENGLAND** INTERNATIONAL WHOSE CLUBS INCLUDED **NEWCASTLE**, **TOTTENHAM HOTSPUR**, **MARSEILLE**, **SHEFFIELD WEDNESDAY**, **BRADFORD CITY**, **SUNDERLAND** AND **BURNLEY**.

THE MONEY MAKERS!

WHEN **ANDY CARROLL** WAS SOLD TO **LIVERPOOL** ON TRANSFER DEADLINE DAY IN 2011, THE £35 MILLION FEE MADE HIM THE MOST EXPENSIVE BRITISH FOOTBALLER OF ALL TIME TO THAT POINT.

IDENTIFY THESE OTHER BIG-MONEY DEPARTURES:

1 AUGUST, 2016: £30 MILLION TO **TOTTENHAM HOTSPUR**

2 JULY, 2014: £12 MILLION TO **ARSENAL**

3 JULY, 1999: £8 MILLION TO **LIVERPOOL**

4 JULY, 2019: £30 MILLION TO **LEICESTER CITY**

5 FEBRUARY, 2009: £6 MILLION TO **MANCHESTER CITY**

6 JULY, 2016: £23 MILLION TO **LIVERPOOL**

7 AUGUST, 2000: £3.75 MILLION TO **EVERTON**

8 JANUARY, 1995: £7 MILLION TO **MANCHESTER UNITED**

9 JANUARY, 2014: £19 MILLION TO **PARIS SAINT-GERMAIN**

10 AUGUST, 2004: £13.4 MILLION TO **REAL MADRID**

11 JULY, 2018: £22 MILLION TO **FULHAM**

12 JANUARY, 2013: £7.65 MILLION TO **CHELSEA**

13 AUGUST, 2008: £12 MILLION TO **ASTON VILLA**

14 AUGUST, 2007: £6 MILLION TO **WEST HAM UNITED**

15 JULY, 2016: £13 MILLION TO **CRYSTAL PALACE**

16 DECEMBER, 1998: £4.4 MILLION TO **LEEDS UNITED**

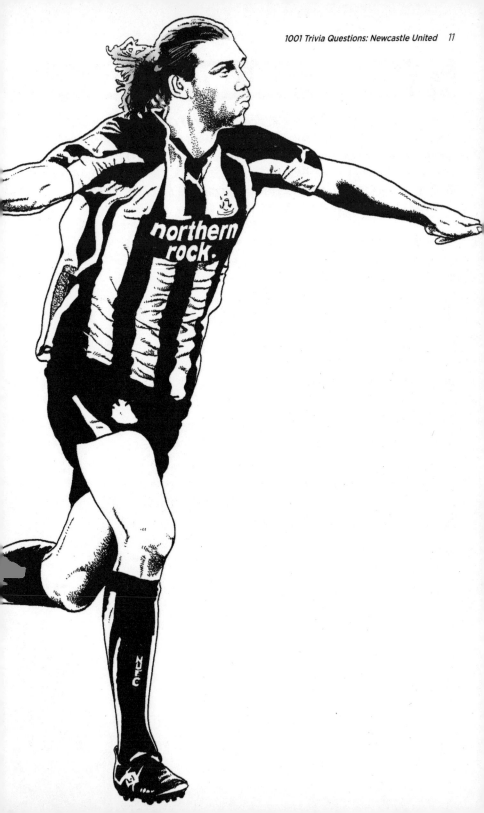

ONES TO WATCH!

BEFORE **NEWCASTLE'S** GAME AGAINST **BRENTFORD** IN NOVEMBER, 2021, FAN-FAVOURITE **ALLAN SAINT-MAXIMIN** GIFTED A £2,000 **TAG HEUER AQUARACER** WATCH TO A FAN WAITING OUTSIDE THE GROUND TO WELCOME THE TEAM! THE **FRANCE** UNDER-21 STAR JOINED **NEWCASTLE** IN 2019 AFTER ESTABLISHING HIS REPUTATION WITH **SAINT-ÉTIENNE, MONACO, HANNOVER 96, BASTIA** AND **NICE.**

FROM WHICH FRENCH CLUBS WERE THE FOLLOWING PLAYERS SIGNED?

1 **RÉMY CABELLA** -- 2014

2 **YOHAN CABAYE** -- 2011

3 **YOAN GOUFFRAN** -- 2013

4 **EMMANUEL RIVIÈRE** -- 2014

5 **FLORIAN THAUVIN** -- 2015

6 **MASSADIO HAIDARA** -- 2013

7 **MAPOU YANGA-MBIW** -- 2013

8 **ROMAIN AMALFITANO** -- 2012

9 **MOUSSA SISSOKO** -- 2013

10 **MATHIEU DEBUCHY** -- 2013

11 **SYLVAIN MARVEAUX** -- 2011

12 **HENRI SAIVET** -- 2016

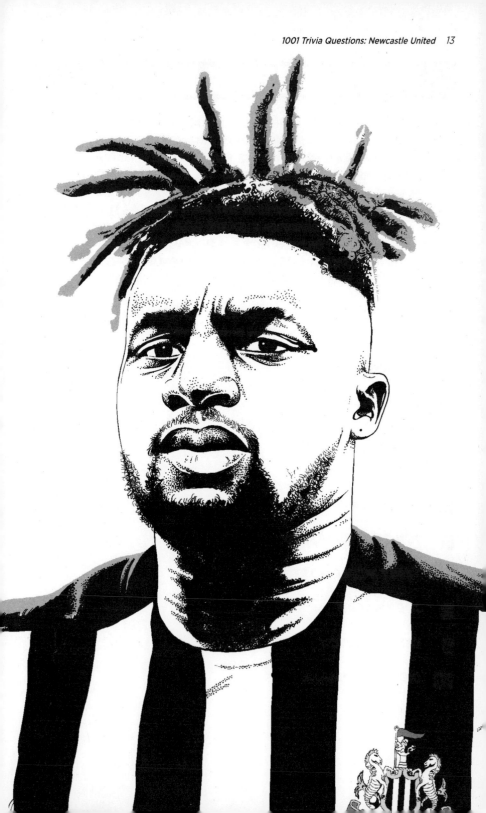

COLOMBIA'S FINEST

HAVING WON THE COPPA ITALIA, THE UEFA CUP AND THE EUROPEAN CUP WINNERS' CUP WITH **PARMA**, WHEN £6.7 MILLION ACQUISITION **FAUSTINO ASPRILLA** ARRIVED AT **ST JAMES' PARK** DURING A SNOWSTORM, THE FLAMBOYANT FORWARD WAS CLAD IN A GIANT FUR COAT. HE MADE HIS DEBUT THE SAME DAY HE SIGNED! HIS PLACE IN GEORDIE FOLKLORE WAS CEMENTED IN 1997 WHEN **NEWCASTLE**, IN THE CLUB'S FIRST-EVER UEFA CHAMPIONS LEAGUE GAME, FACED THE MIGHTY **BARCELONA** ... AND **TINO** BAGGED A HAT-TRICK IN A FAMOUS 3-2 VICTORY! THE **COLOMBIA** STAR RETURNED TO **PARMA** THE FOLLOWING YEAR ... WHERE HE ADDED A SECOND UEFA CUP TO HIS MEDAL HAUL.

WITH WHICH TEAM DID THE FOLLOWING **NEWCASTLE** ALUMNI WIN A UEFA CUP OR UEFA EUROPA LEAGUE WINNER'S MEDAL?

1 KEVIN KEEGAN

2 EMRE BELÖZOĞLU

3 LUUK DE JONG

4 MICHAEL OWEN

5 OSVALDO ARDILES

6 JON DAHL TOMASSON

7 TERRY MCDERMOTT

8 JOE KINNEAR

9 CHRIS HUGHTON

10 DIETMAR HAMANN

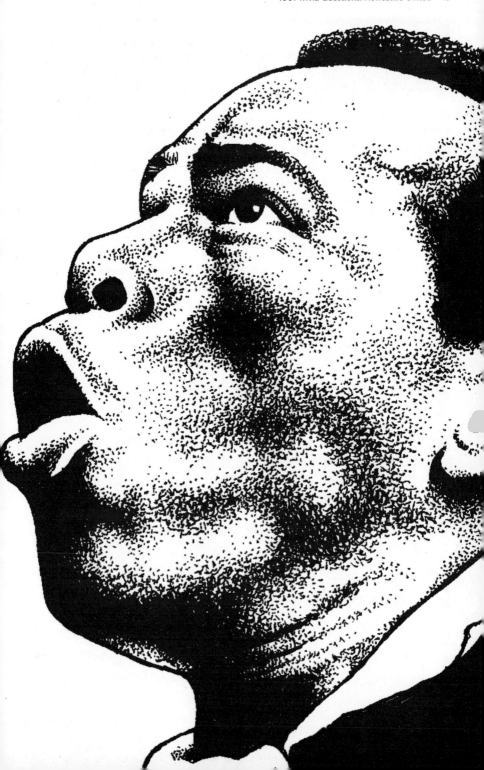

PFA YOUNG PLAYER OF THE YEAR

ALTHOUGH INJURY MEANT THAT HE FEATURED JUST ONCE IN THE LAST THREE MONTHS OF THE 2001-02 PREMIER LEAGUE CAMPAIGN, IN HIS FIRST SEASON WITH **NEWCASTLE**, **CRAIG BELLAMY** SCORED 14 GOALS FOR THE SIDE AND WAS AWARDED THE PFA YOUNG PLAYER OF THE YEAR AWARD.

NAME THESE OTHER **NEWCASTLE** PLAYERS WHO HAVE WON THE AWARD:

1 1982-83: **WALES** INTERNATIONAL WHO WON THE AWARD WHILE PLAYING FOR **LIVERPOOL**.

2 1987-88: **NEWCASTLE** MIDFIELDER IN HIS FINAL SEASON WITH THE CLUB BEFORE HIS BRITISH RECORD TRANSFER.

3 1993-94: **NEWCASTLE** STRIKER WHO ENDED THE SEASON WITH A RECORD 41 GOALS IN ALL COMPETITIONS.

4 1997-98: **ENGLAND** INTERNATIONAL WHO WON THE AWARD WHILE PLAYING FOR **LIVERPOOL**.

5 2002-03: MIDFIELDER WHO WON THE AWARD IN HIS FIRST FULL SEASON WITH **NEWCASTLE** FOLLOWING HIS TRANSFER FROM **NOTTINGHAM FOREST**.

6 2003-04: MIDFIELDER WHO WON THE AWARD IN THE SEASON THAT HE JOINED **CHELSEA** FROM **CHARLTON ATHLETIC** MIDWAY THROUGH THE CAMPAIGN.

7 2009-10: MIDFIELDER WHO WON THE AWARD IN HIS FINAL SEASON WITH **ASTON VILLA** BEFORE JOINING **MANCHESTER CITY**.

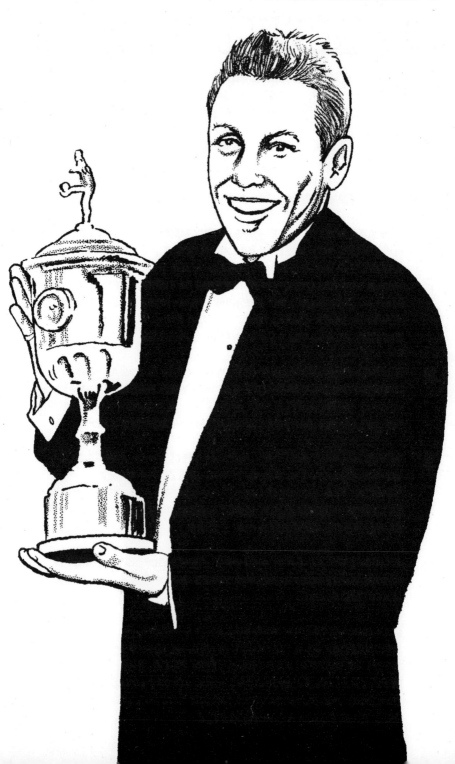

SHEFFIELD STEAL

CHRIS WADDLE JOINED **SHEFFIELD WEDNESDAY** IN THE SUMMER OF 1992 IN A £1 MILLION TRANSFER FROM **MARSEILLE**. HE HELPED THE CLUB REACH BOTH DOMESTIC CUP FINALS THAT SEASON -- THEY LOST TO **ARSENAL** IN EACH -- AND WAS REWARDED WITH THE FOOTBALL WRITERS' ASSOCIATION FOOTBALLER OF THE YEAR AWARD.

NAME THESE OTHERS WHO HAVE PLAYED FOR **NEWCASTLE UNITED** AND **SHEFFIELD WEDNESDAY**:

1 DEFENDER WHO WON A EUROPEAN CUP MEDAL AS AN UNUSED SUBSTITUTE WITH **ASTON VILLA**, HE SPENT A SEASON WITH **SHEFFIELD WEDNESDAY**, DURING WHICH TIME HE WAS FORCED TO TAKE A TAXI TO LONDON FOR THE 1983 FA CUP SEMI-FINAL HAVING BEEN ACCIDENTALLY LEFT BEHIND BY TEAM BOSS **JACK CHARLTON**. HOWEVER, WHEN **CHARLTON** TOOK THE REINS AT **NEWCASTLE UNITED**, HE WAS THE NEW MANAGER'S FIRST SIGNING.

2 JOURNEYMAN FORWARD WHO PLAYED FOR 16 CLUBS AT VARIOUS LEVELS, HE WON A PROMOTION IN 1984 WITH **WEDNESDAY** AFTER LEAVING **NEWCASTLE** AND WAS LATER INSTRUMENTAL IN INSPIRING THE INFLATABLE BANANA CRAZE AT **MANCHESTER CITY**.

3 MIDFIELDER WHO HAD TWO LENGTHY SPELLS WITH **SHEFFIELD WEDNESDAY** IN THE 1980S, EITHER SIDE OF HIS TIME AT **NEWCASTLE**. HE SUBSEQUENTLY MANAGED A NUMBER OF TEAMS INCLUDING **WEDNESDAY, WEST BROM, BOLTON, LEICESTER, BLACKPOOL, NORWICH** AND **STOKE**.

4 **MOROCCO** FULL-BACK WHO WAS LOANED OUT TO **SHEFFIELD WEDNESDAY** DURING HIS FIVE YEARS ON TYNESIDE. HE JOINED **WATFORD** IN 2021.

5 SCOTTISH MIDFIELDER WHO WAS A CLUB RECORD SIGNING TO **WEDNESDAY** AS A TEENAGER IN 1968, HE JOINED **NEWCASTLE** IN 1974. HE LATER PLAYED FOR **ASTON VILLA, SWANSEA CITY, CARLISLE UNITED** AND **HIBS**, BEFORE EMBARKING ON A COACHING AND MANAGEMENT CAREER THAT INCLUDED A SPELL AS FIRST TEAM COACH AT **NEWCASTLE**.

6 JAMAICA-BORN WINGER WHO SPENT MUCH OF HIS SEVEN YEARS WITH *NEWCASTLE* OUT ON LOAN, INCLUDING A SPELL WITH *SHEFFIELD WEDNESDAY* IN 2019. HE SIGNED FOR *HUDDERSFIELD TOWN* IN 2021.

7 *ENGLAND'S* FIRST £500,000 FOOTBALLER WHEN HE JOINED *WEST BROM* FROM *MIDDLESBROUGH* IN 1979, HIS SUBSEQUENT CLUBS INCLUDED *WEDNESDAY*, *NEWCASTLE*, A RETURN TO *MIDDLESBROUGH* AND *DARLINGTON*.

8 *ENGLAND* INTERNATIONAL NICKNAMED *"THE MAN WITH THE FLUTTERING FEET"*, AN INSIDE-FORWARD WHO LEFT *NEWCASTLE* FOR *SHEFFIELD WEDNESDAY* IN 1932 AND CAPTAINED *"THE OWLS"* TO VICTORY IN THE 1935 FA CUP FINAL.

9 *ENGLAND U-21* WINGER WHO LAUNCHED HIS CAREER WITH *NORWICH CITY* BEFORE SIGNING FOR *NEWCASTLE* IN 2017. HE HAS SUBSEQUENTLY SPENT TIME ON LOAN AT *WEST BROM* AND *SHEFFIELD WEDNESDAY*.

10 SCOTLAND WINGER WHO PLAYED FOR *DUNFERMLINE ATHLETIC* AND *LEICESTER CITY*, WON THE 1969 INTER-CITIES FAIRS CUP WITH *NEWCASTLE*, SPENT FOUR YEARS WITH *SHEFFIELD WEDNESDAY* AND RETURNED TO *DUNFERMLINE* IN 1973.

GREECE IS THE WORD

A LEGEND ON TYNESIDE FOR THE GOAL HE SCORED IN THE 1-0 DERBY WIN OVER **SUNDERLAND** AT THE **STADIUM OF LIGHT** IN 2002, **NIKOS DABIZAS** PLAYED IN TWO CUP FINALS FOR **"THE MAGPIES"** BEFORE JOINING **LEICESTER CITY** IN EARLY 2004. LATER THAT YEAR, HE WAS A MEMBER OF THE VICTORIOUS **GREECE** SQUAD AT EURO 2004.

IDENTIFY THESE OTHERS WHO HAVE PLAYED FOR **NEWCASTLE UNITED** AND **LEICESTER CITY.**

1 THE 2013 ALGERIAN FOOTBALLER OF THE YEAR, HE BECAME **LEICESTER CITY'S** RECORD SIGNING WHEN HE JOINED FROM **SPORTING CP** IN 2015. HE SPENT TIME ON LOAN AT **NEWCASTLE,** **FENERBAHÇE** AND **MONACO** BEFORE JOINING **LYON** IN 2021.

2 CAPPED 86 TIMES BY **NORTHERN IRELAND,** WINGER WHOSE CLUBS INCLUDE **MANCHESTER UNITED, NEWCASTLE, BLACKBURN, LEICESTER, SHEFFIELD UNITED** AND MORE.

3 **ENGLAND** CENTRE-BACK WHO WON FIRST DIVISION TITLES WITH **NEWCASTLE** AND **MANCHESTER CITY,** EITHER SIDE OF A SEASON WITH **LEICESTER CITY** IN 2003-04.

4 **SPAIN U21** FORWARD WHO SPENT FIVE YEARS AT **NEWCASTLE** BEFORE JOINING **LEICESTER** IN A £30 MILLION DEAL IN 2019.

5 A MEMBER OF THE **WALES** 1958 WORLD CUP SQUAD, HE SCORED IN EVERY ROUND OF THE FA CUP IN 1961 FOR **LEICESTER** BUT WAS DROPPED FOR THE FINAL, FOLLOWING WHICH HE SIGNED FOR **NEWCASTLE.** SUBSEQUENT CLUBS INCLUDED **BIRMINGHAM CITY, NORTHAMPTON TOWN** AND **BRADFORD CITY.**

6 THE FIRST PERUVIAN TO PLAY IN THE PREMIER LEAGUE, AND THE FIRST TO APPEAR IN THE FA CUP FINAL.

7 **ENGLAND** STRIKER WHO WON HONOURS WITH **BEŞIKTAŞ** AND **TOTTENHAM HOTSPUR,** AND PLAYED FOR A NUMBER OF CLUBS, INCLUDING **QPR, NEWCASTLE, WEST HAM UNITED, LEICESTER, BOLTON, READING** AND **WATFORD.**

8   HAVING LAUNCHED HIS CAREER AT *LEICESTER CITY* IN 1989, STRIKER WHO PLAYED FOR *DERBY COUNTY, NEWCASTLE, WEST HAM, CHARLTON ATHLETIC, CRYSTAL PALACE, BRIGHTON & HOVE ALBION* AND MORE.

9   *MANCHESTER UNITED* YOUTH GRADUATE WHO WON CHAMPIONSHIP TITLES WITH *SUNDERLAND* AND *NEWCASTLE* AND A PROMOTION WITH *QPR* BEFORE JOINING *LEICESTER CITY* IN 2014, WITH WHOM HE WON A PREMIER LEAGUE TITLE IN 2016. HE HAS SUBSEQUENTLY PLAYED FOR *HUDDERSFIELD TOWN* AND *BRISTOL CITY*.

A GALLIC GREAT

THE 1993 FRENCH PLAYER OF THE YEAR, **DAVID GINOLA** WON LEAGUE AND CUP HONOURS WITH **PARIS SAINT-GERMAIN** BEFORE SIGNING FOR **NEWCASTLE** IN 1995. THE FOLLOWING YEAR, **"THE MAGPIES"** TURNED DOWN A £15 MILLION OFFER FROM **BOBBY ROBSON'S BARCELONA** ... BUT WHEN **KENNY DALGLISH** REPLACED **KEVIN KEEGAN** AS **NEWCASTLE** MANAGER, **GINOLA** FELL OUT OF FAVOUR AND WAS SOLD TO **TOTTENHAM HOTSPUR** IN THE SUMMER OF 1997 FOR £2.5 MILLION.

NAME THESE OTHER **KEVIN KEEGAN** SIGNINGS DURING HIS TWO TERMS AS **NEWCASTLE** MANAGER:

1 JULY, 1996: £15 MILLION FROM **BLACKBURN ROVERS**

2 JUNE, 1995: £6 MILLION FROM **QUEENS PARK RANGERS**

3 FEBRUARY, 1996: £6.7 MILLION FROM **PARMA**

4 FEBRUARY, 1996: £3.75 MILLION FROM **BLACKBURN ROVERS**

5 MARCH, 1994: £2.7 MILLION FROM **QUEENS PARK RANGERS**

6 JUNE, 1995: £4 MILLION FROM **WIMBLEDON**

7 SEPTEMBER, 1994: £2.25 MILLION FROM **DERBY COUNTY**

8 FEBRUARY, 1993: £1.75 MILLION FROM **BRISTOL CITY**

9 FEBRUARY, 1994: £2.25 MILLION FROM **NORWICH CITY**

10 JULY, 1995: £1.575 MILLION FROM **READING**

11 JULY, 1993: £1.5 MILLION FROM **EVERTON**

12 AUGUST, 1992: £700,000 FROM **CHARLTON ATHLETIC**

13 AUGUST, 2008: £10.3 MILLION FROM **DEPORTIVO DE LA CORUÑA**

14 JULY, 2008: £5.22 MILLION FROM **MALLORCA**

15 JULY, 2008: £2.5 MILLION
FROM *LIVERPOOL*

16 JULY, 2008: £500,000
FROM *METZ*

HOWE-WAY THE LADS!

EDDIE HOWE SPENT MOST OF HIS PLAYING CAREER AT **BOURNEMOUTH**, MAKING 300 APPEARANCES DURING TWO SPELLS AT THE CLUB. APPOINTED **BOURNEMOUTH** MANAGER IN 2008, HE STEERED THE CLUB TO PROMOTION TO LEAGUE ONE BEFORE JOINING **BURNLEY** IN 2011. HE RETURNED TO **BOURNEMOUTH** THE FOLLOWING YEAR AND LED THE CLUB TO PROMOTION TO THE CHAMPIONSHIP AND THEN THE PREMIER LEAGUE. HE LEFT **BOURNEMOUTH** FOLLOWING RELEGATION IN 2020. HE WAS APPOINTED NEWCASTLE MANAGER IN NOVEMBER, 2021.

WHICH **NEWCASTLE** BOSS MANAGED:

1 SWINDON TOWN, WEST BROMWICH ALBION, TOTTENHAM HOTSPUR, GUADALAJARA, SHIMIZU S-PULSE, CROATIA ZAGREB, YOKOHAMA F. MARINOS, AL-ITTIHAD SC ALEPPO, RACING CLUB, TOKYO VERDY, BEITAR JERUSALEM, HURACÁN, CERRO PORTEÑO, FC MACHIDA ZELVIA

2 READING, WEST HAM UNITED, CHARLTON ATHLETIC, SOUTHAMPTON, CRYSTAL PALACE, WEST BROMWICH ALBION, ADO DEN HAAG

3 INDIA, NEPAL, DONCASTER ROVERS (CARETAKER), WIMBLEDON, NOTTINGHAM FOREST

4 COLERAINE, GUAM

5 GILLINGHAM, WATFORD, WEST HAM UNITED, NORWICH CITY, STEVENAGE

6 VANCOUVER ROYALS, FULHAM, IPSWICH TOWN, ENGLAND, PSV EINDHOVEN, SPORTING CP, PORTO, BARCELONA

7 CROOK TOWN, BARROW, WORKINGTON

8 SHEFFIELD UNITED, HUDDERSFIELD TOWN, WIGAN ATHLETIC, CRYSTAL PALACE, BIRMINGHAM CITY, SUNDERLAND, HULL CITY, ASTON VILLA, SHEFFIELD WEDNESDAY

9 *MIDDLESBROUGH, SHEFFIELD WEDNESDAY, REPUBLIC OF IRELAND*

10 *CHESTERFIELD, DERBY COUNTY*

ENGLAND EXPECTS

KEVIN KEEGAN MADE 63 APPEARANCES FOR **ENGLAND**, 31 OF THEM AS CAPTAIN ... BUT HE MANAGED ONLY ONE WORLD CUP APPEARANCE. AFTER **ENGLAND** FAILED TO QUALIFY FOR THE 1974 AND 1978 TOURNAMENTS, HE WAS NAMED IN THE 1982 SQUAD FOR THE TOURNAMENT, BUT A CHRONIC BACK INJURY RULED HIM OUT OF ALL OF **ENGLAND'S** GROUP GAMES. HE SECRETLY HIRED A CAR AND DROVE FROM SPAIN TO A SPECIALIST HE KNEW IN GERMANY FOR INTENSIVE TREATMENT. HE RECOVERED SUFFICIENTLY TO APPEAR AS A SUBSTITUTE FOR THE LAST 26 MINUTES OF THE SECOND-ROUND GAME AGAINST HOSTS **SPAIN**, A GAME **ENGLAND** NEEDED TO WIN TO PROGRESS TO THE SEMI-FINALS. **KEEGAN** MISSED A POINT-BLANK HEADER WHICH WOULD HAVE BROKEN THE DEADLOCK, THE GAME ENDED 0-0 AND **ENGLAND** WERE ELIMINATED FROM THE COMPETITION.

IDENTIFY THESE **ENGLAND** INTERNATIONAL **NEWCASTLE** PLAYERS:

1 89 CAPS BETWEEN 1998 AND 2008 WHILE PLAYING FOR **LIVERPOOL, REAL MADRID** AND **NEWCASTLE**

2 86 CAPS BETWEEN 1979 AND 1988 WHILE PLAYING FOR **CRYSTAL PALACE** AND **ARSENAL**

3 79 CAPS BETWEEN 1983 AND 1995 WHILE PLAYING FOR **WATFORD** AND **LIVERPOOL**

4 78 CAPS BETWEEN 1987 AND 1999 WHILE PLAYING FOR **NOTTINGHAM FOREST** AND **WEST HAM UNITED**

5 73 CAPS BETWEEN 1996 AND 2007 WHILE PLAYING FOR **TOTTENHAM HOTSPUR, ARSENAL** AND **PORTSMOUTH**

6 63 CAPS BETWEEN 1992 AND 2000 WHILE PLAYING FOR *SOUTHAMPTON, BLACKBURN* AND *NEWCASTLE*

7 62 CAPS BETWEEN 1985 AND 1991 WHILE PLAYING FOR *NEWCASTLE, TOTTENHAM HOTSPUR* AND *MARSEILLE*

8 61 CAPS BETWEEN 2009 AND 2016 WHILE PLAYING FOR *ASTON VILLA, MANCHESTER CITY* AND *LIVERPOOL*

9 59 CAPS BETWEEN 1986 AND 1996 WHILE PLAYING FOR *NEWCASTLE* AND *LIVERPOOL*

10 57 CAPS BETWEEN 1998 AND 2008 WHILE PLAYING FOR *TOTTENHAM, LAZIO, RANGERS* AND *MIDDLESBROUGH*

HEY, BIG SPENDER!

BRAZIL U-17 FORWARD **JOELINTON** JOINED **NEWCASTLE** FROM GERMANY'S **1899 HOFFENHEIM** IN THE SUMMER OF 2019, THE £40 MILLION TRANSFER FEE SET A NEW CLUB RECORD,

FROM WHICH CLUBS WERE THESE BIG MONEY PLAYERS SIGNED?

1 **CALLUM WILSON** -- £20 MILLION

2 **MIGUEL ALMIRÓN** -- £21 MILLION

3 **ALLAN SAINT-MAXIMIN** -- £16.5 MILLION

4 **OBAFEMI MARTINS** -- £15 MILLION

5 **ALAN SHEARER** -- £15 MILLION

6 **GEORGINIO WIJNALDUM** -- £14.5 MILLION

7 **JAMAL LEWIS** -- £15 MILLION

8 **ALEKSANDAR MITROVIĆ** -- £13 MILLION

9 **FLORIAN THAUVIN** -- £15 MILLION

10 **JOE WILLOCK** -- £25 MILLION

11 **DWIGHT GAYLE** -- £10 MILLION

12 **MICHAEL OWEN** -- £16.8 MILLION

13 **MATT RITCHIE** -- £10 MILLION

14 **ANDROS TOWNSEND** -- £12 MILLION

15 **JONJO SHELVEY** -- £12 MILLION

16 **JACOB MURPHY** -- £12 MILLION

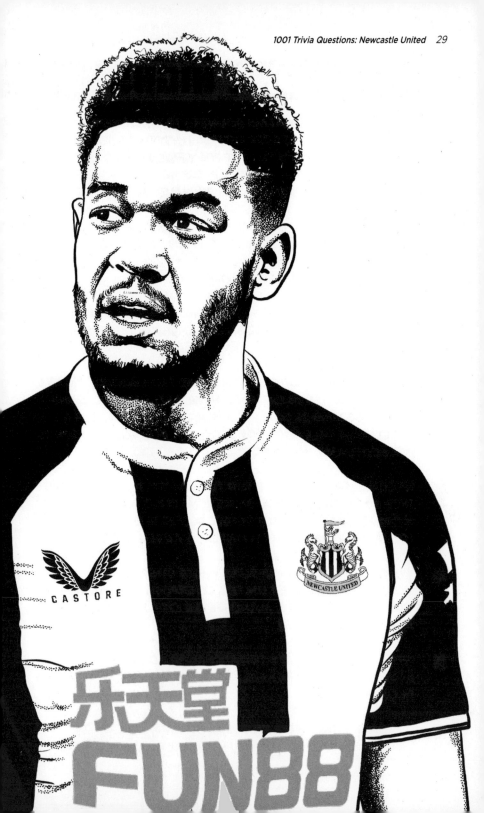

ALL-TIME HIGHS

PERSUADED BY MANAGER *GRAEME SOUNESS* TO SHELVE HIS PLANS
FOR RETIREMENT, *ALAN SHEARER* ENTERED THE 2005-06 SEASON
CHASING *JACKIE MILBURN'S* TALLY OF 200 *NEWCASTLE* GOALS, A
RECORD THAT HAD STOOD FOR 49 YEARS. IN THE PREMIER LEAGUE HOME
FIXTURE AGAINST *PORTSMOUTH* ON FEBRUARY 4, 2006, HE SCORED HIS
201ST GOAL FOR THE CLUB. TEN WEEKS LATER, A SERIOUS KNEE INJURY
CURTAILED HIS SEASON AND HASTENED HIS RETIREMENT, HAVING SCORED
A TOTAL OF 206 GOALS IN ALL COMPETITIONS FOR *"THE MAGPIES".*

IDENTIFY THESE *NEWCASTLE* GOALSCORING GREATS:

1 153 GOALS: SIGNED FOR £12,500 FROM *ROTHERHAM UNITED*, HE
SPENT A DECADE ON TYNESIDE BEFORE JOINING *HUDDERSFIELD
TOWN* IN 1962.

2 143 GOALS: PROLIFIC GOALSCORER SIGNED FROM *AIRDRIEONIANS*
FOR £6,500 IN 1925, HE CAPTAINED *NEWCASTLE* THE FOLLOWING
SEASON, SCORING 36 GOALS IN 38 GAMES TO GIVE THE CLUB A
FIRST LEAGUE TITLE SINCE 1909. SCORER OF 24 GOALS IN 20 GAMES
FOR *SCOTLAND*, HE MOVED TO *CHELSEA* IN 1930.

3 121 GOALS: SIGNED FROM *LUTON TOWN* IN 1971, HE BAGGED A HAT-
TRICK AGAINST *LIVERPOOL* ON HIS HOME DEBUT. AN *ENGLAND*
INTERNATIONAL, HE WAS TOP LEAGUE SCORER IN 1975 AND --
FOLLOWING A £333,333.34 TRANSFER TO *ARSENAL* -- IN 1977,

4 119 GOALS: *ENGLAND* MIDFIELDER WHOSE OTHER CLUBS
INCLUDED *MANCHESTER UNITED, LIVERPOOL, EVERTON,
BOLTON WANDERERS, MANCHESTER CITY, FULHAM* AND
HARTLEPOOL UNITED.

5 113 GOALS: *SCOTLAND* INTERNATIONAL, HE WON THREE FA CUPS IN
A FIVE-YEAR PERIOD, WHICH INCLUDED SCORING A GOAL IN THE 1955
FA CUP FINAL.

6 113 GOALS: SIGNED FROM *RANGERS*, DURING HIS DECADE ON
TYNESIDE HE WON THE 1924 FA CUP AND THE LEAGUE TITLE IN 1927.

7   101 GOALS: SCORED THE OPENING GOAL IN THE 1924 FA CUP FINAL.

8   97 GOALS: HAVING LAUNCHED HIS CAREER AT **NEWCASTLE**, HE HAD TWO SPELLS AT **WEST HAM** AND THREE SPELLS AT BOTH **SUNDERLAND** AND **CARLISLE UNITED** -- TWO TEAMS HE SUBSEQUENTLY MANAGED!

PAYING THEIR DUES

JACK CHARLTON SPENT HIS ENTIRE PLAYING CAREER WITH *LEEDS UNITED* FROM 1950 TO 1973, HELPING THE CLUB TO A SECOND DIVISION TITLE, FIRST DIVISION TITLE, FA CUP, LEAGUE CUP AND TWO INTER-CITIES FAIRS CUPS. HIS 629 LEAGUE AND 762 TOTAL COMPETITIVE APPEARANCES ARE CLUB RECORDS.

IDENTIFY THESE OTHER *NEWCASTLE UNITED* MANAGERS -- INCLUDING CARETAKER MANAGERS -- BY THE CLUBS THEY PLAYED FOR:

1   *SOUTHAMPTON, BLACKBURN ROVERS, NEWCASTLE UNITED*

2   *WHYTELEAFE, EPSOM & EWELL, CORINTHIAN-CASUALS, DULWICH HAMLET, YEOVIL TOWN, CRYSTAL PALACE, CHARLTON ATHLETIC, TOTTENHAM HOTSPUR, BARNET, READING*

3   *HFC HAARLEM, FEYENOORD, PSV, AC MILAN, SAMPDORIA, CHELSEA*

4   *WOLVERHAMPTON WANDERERS, BOURNEMOUTH & BOSCOMBE ATHLETIC, BRADFORD CITY, NEWCASTLE UNITED*

5   *BEITH JUNIORS, ST MIRREN, CHELSEA*

6   *TOTTENHAM HOTSPUR, MONTREAL OLYMPIQUE, MIDDLESBROUGH, WEST ADELAIDE, LIVERPOOL, SAMPDORIA, RANGERS*

7   *REAL MADRID AFICIONADOS, REAL MADRID CASTILLA, PARLA, LINARES*

8   *FULHAM, WEST BROMWICH ALBION, VANCOUVER ROYALS*

9   *SUNDERLAND, WEST BROMWICH ALBION, NORWICH CITY*

10   *LINFIELD*

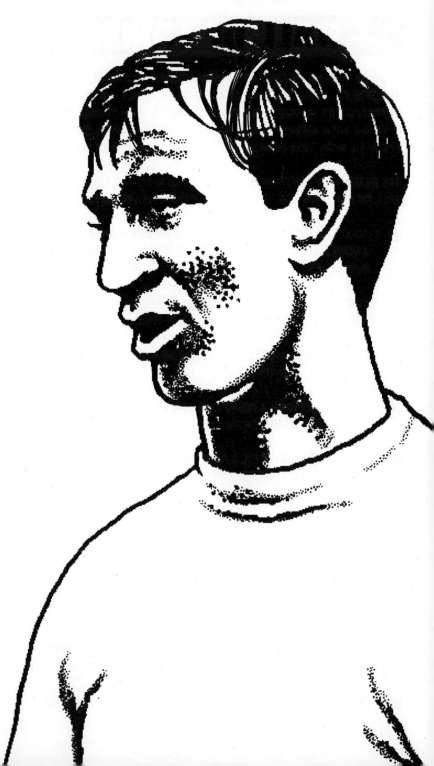

HALL OF FAMERS

GEORDIE LEGEND *JACKIE MILBURN* SCORED 200 GOALS FOR *"THE MAGPIES"*, A RECORD THAT STOOD FOR 49 YEARS UNTIL IT WAS SURPASSED BY *ALAN SHEARER* IN 2006. HE WON THREE FA CUPS IN HIS 12 YEARS WITH *NEWCASTLE*, BEFORE JOINING *LINFIELD* IN 1957, WITH WHOM HE WON TWO IRISH LEAGUE CHAMPIONSHIPS AND THE IRISH CUP.

MILBURN WAS POSTHUMOUSLY INDUCTED INTO THE ENGLISH FOOTBALL HALL OF FAME IN 2006. NAME THESE OTHER *NEWCASTLE* INDUCTEES:

1 2002: *NEWCASTLE UNITED, TOTTENHAM HOTSPUR, MIDDLESBROUGH, EVERTON, BURNLEY, BOSTON UNITED* DURING 1985-2004

2 2002: *SCUNTHORPE UNITED, LIVERPOOL, SOUTHAMPTON, NEWCASTLE UNITED* DURING 1968-1984

3 2004: *SOUTHAMPTON, BLACKBURN ROVERS, NEWCASTLE UNITED* DURING 1998-2006

4 2004: *WATFORD, LIVERPOOL, NEWCASTLE UNITED, CHARLTON ATHLETIC* DURING 1981-1999

5 2006: *CHESTER CITY, LIVERPOOL, LEEDS UNITED, NEWCASTLE UNITED, SHEFFIELD UNITED, WREXHAM* DURING 1978-1999

6 2007: *CARLISLE UNITED, NEWCASTLE UNITED, LIVERPOOL, EVERTON, BOLTON WANDERERS, MANCHESTER CITY, FULHAM, HARTLEPOOL UNITED* DURING 1979-1999

7 2009: *BRADFORD PARK AVENUE, NEWCASTLE UNITED, SUNDERLAND* DURING 1940-1957

8 2014: *NEWCASTLE UNITED, CHELSEA, DERBY COUNTY, NOTTS COUNTY, GRIMSBY TOWN, GATESHEAD* DURING 1925-1939

9 2014: *LIVERPOOL, NEWCASTLE UNITED, MANCHESTER UNITED, STOKE CITY* DURING 1996-2013

10 2015: *SWANSEA TOWN, NEWCASTLE UNITED, CARDIFF CITY* DURING 1949-1968

11 2015: *COVENTRY CITY, NOTTINGHAM FOREST, NEWCASTLE UNITED, WEST HAM UNITED, MANCHESTER CITY* DURING 1983-2002

12 2017: *LEEDS UNITED, EVERTON, NEWCASTLE UNITED, BOLTON WANDERERS, SHEFFIELD UNITED* DURING 1988-2010

VILLAINS!

THE ARRIVAL OF *NOLBERTO SOLANO* FROM *ASTON VILLA* IN 2005 SAW *JAMES MILNER* GO IN THE OTHER DIRECTION ON LOAN FOR THE REST OF THE SEASON. DESPITE *VILLA'S* ATTEMPTS TO MAKE THE DEAL PERMANENT, *MILNER* PLAYED IN *NEWCASTLE* COLOURS THE FOLLOWING SEASON ... BUT *VILLA* RETURNED WITH A SUCCESSFUL £12 MILLION BID IN AUGUST, 2008.

IDENTIFY THESE OTHERS WHO HAVE PLAYED FOR BOTH *NEWCASTLE UNITED* AND *ASTON VILLA*:

1 *REPUBLIC OF IRELAND* GOALKEEPER WHO JOINED *VILLA* IN 2011 AFTER THREE SEASONS WITH *MANCHESTER CITY*.

2 FRENCH WINGER WHO LEFT *NEWCASTLE* FOR *WIGAN ATHLETIC* IN EARLY 2009 AND JOINED *ASTON VILLA* 18 MONTHS LATER.

3 CAPPED 112 TIMES BY *NORTHERN IRELAND*, DEFENDER WHO MADE 278 APPEARANCES FOR *"THE MAGPIES"* BEFORE HIS CAREER TOOK HIM TO *ASTON VILLA*, *FULHAM*, *QPR*, *BRIGHTON* AND TEAMS IN AUSTRALIA, INDIA AND SCOTLAND.

4 THE 1993 FRENCH PLAYER OF THE YEAR AND WINNER OF BOTH ENGLISH POTY AWARDS IN 1999.

5 WINGER WHO, HAVING PLAYED FOR *CRYSTAL PALACE*, *SPURS*, *PORTSMOUTH*, *FULHAM*, *ASTON VILLA* AND *CARDIFF CITY*, HELPED *NEWCASTLE* WIN THE FOOTBALL LEAGUE CHAMPIONSHIP IN 2010, *QPR* WIN THE SAME TROPHY IN 2011 AND FINALLY WIN THE LEAGUE CUP WITH *SWANSEA CITY* IN 2013.

6 JOURNEYMAN STRIKER WHO SCORED FIVE GOALS IN 15 GAMES FOR *NEWCASTLE* ON LOAN FROM *VILLA* IN 2009, HIS OTHER CLUBS INCLUDE *NOTTINGHAM FOREST*, *IPSWICH TOWN*, *WEST HAM*, *WOLVES*, *BLACKPOOL*, *BARNSLEY* AND MORE.

7 FAI YOUNG INTERNATIONAL PLAYER OF THE YEAR IN 2007, WHOSE INTERNATIONAL CAREER CAME TO AN ABRUPT HALT IN CONTROVERSIAL CIRCUMSTANCES, HE LEFT *MANCHESTER CITY* FOR *ASTON VILLA* IN A SWAP DEAL INVOLVING *JAMES MILNER*. A SUBSEQUENT LOAN TO *NEWCASTLE* WAS CURTAILED BY INJURY.

8 WINGER WHO WON TWO LEAGUE CUPS WITH *NOTTINGHAM FOREST*, HE JOINED *NEWCASTLE* IN 1991 FOR £250,000, SUBSEQUENT CLUBS INCLUDED *SHEFFIELD UNITED*, *LEICESTER*, *ASTON VILLA*, *BOLTON* AND *WEST BROM*.

9 SIGNED FROM *MARSEILLE* IN 2007, FRENCH RIGHT-BACK WHO WAS CAPPED 35 TIMES BY *SENEGAL*, HE MOVED ON TO *ASTON VILLA* FOLLOWING RELEGATION IN 2009.

10 *REPUBLIC OF IRELAND* DEFENDER SIGNED FROM *VILLA* IN 2016.

11 CAPPED 62 TIMES BY *NORWAY*, DEFENDER WHO WON THE UEFA CHAMPIONS LEAGUE AND THREE PREMIER LEAGUE TITLES WITH *MANCHESTER UNITED* BEFORE SPENDING TWO SEASONS AT *ASTON VILLA*. HE PLAYED A HANDFUL OF GAMES FOR *NEWCASTLE* BUT WAS RELEASED OVER FITNESS LEVELS.

12 STRIKER WHO WON THE LEAGUE AND LEAGUE CUP WITH *NOTTINGHAM FOREST*, THE LEAGUE AND EUROPEAN CUP WITH *ASTON VILLA* AND LATER SCORED 25 GOALS IN 78 GAMES FOR *NEWCASTLE* BETWEEN 1978 AND 1980.

BLUE AND WHITE HOOPS, BLACK AND WHITE STRIPES

LES FERDINAND PLAYED NON-LEAGUE FOOTBALL UNTIL HE WAS 20 YEARS OLD, WHEN HE WAS SPOTTED AND SIGNED BY **QUEENS PARK RANGERS**. HE WENT ON TO WIN 17 **ENGLAND** CAPS AND BANG IN GOALS FOR **NEWCASTLE, SPURS** AND **LEICESTER CITY** AMONG OTHERS.

IDENTIFY THESE OTHERS WHO HAVE PLAYED FOR **NEWCASTLE** AND **QPR**:

1 CENTRAL DEFENDER SIGNED FROM **QPR** IN EARLY 1994. HE MADE 176 APPEARANCES FOR THE CLUB BEFORE JOINING **BLACKBURN ROVERS** IN 1998. HE SUFFERED A SERIOUS NECK INJURY WHILE ON LOAN AT **WOLVES** THAT ENDED HIS CAREER AT THE AGE OF 32.

2 CONTROVERSIAL MIDFIELDER SIGNED FROM **MANCHESTER CITY** IN 2007, HE WON HONOURS WITH **NEWCASTLE, QPR** AND **BURNLEY**, AND PLAYED IN FRANCE AND SCOTLAND IN A CAREER MARKED BY VIOLENT INCIDENTS ON AND OFF THE FIELD.

3 CAPPED 86 TIMES BY **ENGLAND**, FULL-BACK WHO WON HONOURS WITH **CRYSTAL PALACE** AND **ARSENAL** BEFORE MOVING ON TO **NEWCASTLE, QPR, COVENTRY CITY, EVERTON, BRENTFORD** AND **WATFORD**.

4 STRIKER CAPPED 31 TIMES BY **NORTHERN IRELAND**, HE WON A SECOND DIVISION TITLE WITH **QPR** BEFORE JOINING **NEWCASTLE** IN 1985.

5 CAPPED 30 TIMES BY *FRANCE*, FORWARD WHO WON HONOURS WITH *LYON* AND *MARSEILLE* BEFORE JOINING *QPR*, WHOSE SUBSEQUENT RELEGATION SAW HIM LOANED TO *NEWCASTLE* IN 2013. HE WON HONOURS WITH *CHELSEA*, SPENT TIME ON LOAN AT *CRYSTAL PALACE* AND HAS SUBSEQUENTLY PLAYED IN SPAIN, FRANCE AND TURKEY.

6 WINGER WHO WON CHAMPIONSHIPS WITH *NEWCASTLE* AND *QPR* AND THE 2014 LEAGUE CUP WITH *SWANSEA CITY*, HAVING PREVIOUSLY PLAYED FOR *CRYSTAL PALACE*, *SPURS*, *PORTSMOUTH*, *FULHAM*, *ASTON VILLA* AND *CARDIFF CITY*.

7 DEFENDER WHOSE CAREER TOOK HIM FROM *BARNET* TO *CHESHAM UNITED*, *OLDHAM ATHLETIC*, *SOUTHAMPTON*, *CRYSTAL PALACE* AND *WIGAN ATHLETIC* BEFORE JOINING *QPR*. HE WON A CHAMPIONSHIP WITH *NEWCASTLE* IN 2010, BEFORE RETURNING TO *QPR* AND WINNING THE CHAMPIONSHIP IN 2011. HE ENDED HIS PLAYING DAYS WITH *WATFORD*.

NOBBY FROM LIMA

DUBBED **"MAESTRITO"** -- **"THE LITTLE MAESTRO"** -- BY **DIEGO MARADONA** AND KNOWN TO THE LEGIONS OF ADORING GEORDIES AS **"NOBBY"**, MIDFIELDER **NOLBERTO SOLANO** WAS THE FIRST PERUVIAN TO PLAY IN THE PREMIER LEAGUE. HE HAD TWO SPELLS WITH **NEWCASTLE** -- EITHER SIDE OF THREE SEASONS WITH **ASTON VILLA** -- SCORING 48 GOALS IN A TOTAL OF 314 APPEARANCES.

SOLANO PLAYED 95 TIMES FOR **PERU.** FOR WHICH COUNTRY WERE THE FOLLOWING PLAYERS CAPPED AS FULL INTERNATIONALS?

1 MIRANDINHA

2 GEORGE ROBLEDO

3 OGUCHI ONYEWU

4 DIEGO GAVILÁN

5 NACHO GONZÁLEZ

6 SALOMÓN RONDÓN

7 EMMANUEL RIVIÈRE

8 SHAKA HISLOP

9 CARL CORT

10 DAVID EDGAR

11 CLARENCE ACUÑA

12 CAÇAPA

13 FAUSTINO ASPRILLA

14 RUEL FOX

15 DEANDRE YEDLIN

COTTAGERS

WHEN **MALCOLM MACDONALD** LEFT **FULHAM** FOR **NEWCASTLE** IN 1971, HE WAS DRIVEN TO HIS NEW CLUB IN A ROLLS-ROYCE. HE SCORED A HAT-TRICK AGAINST **LIVERPOOL** ON HIS HOME DEBUT AND WAS IMMEDIATELY DUBBED **"SUPERMAC"** BY THE ADORING GEORDIE FAITHFUL!

1 **BELGIUM** INTERNATIONAL WHO WON MULTIPLE HONOURS WITH **KV MECHELEN** AND **ANDERLECHT**, HE JOINED **NEWCASTLE** IN 1995. TOWARDS THE END OF HIS STAY ON TYNESIDE, HE WAS LOANED OUT TO **FULHAM** WHERE HE PLAYED UNDER FORMER BOSS **KEVIN KEEGAN** AND HELPED SECURE A DIVISION TWO CHAMPIONSHIP IN 1999.

2 **SERBIA** STRIKER SIGNED FROM **ANDERLECHT** IN 2015, HE WON THE CHAMPIONSHIP WITH **NEWCASTLE** IN 2017 BEFORE MAKING A LOAN MOVE TO **FULHAM** PERMANENT IN 2018. IN FOUR SEASONS HE EXPERIENCED TWO PROMOTIONS TO THE PREMIER LEAGUE, EACH FOLLOWED BY IMMEDIATE RELEGATION.

3 CAPPED TWICE BY **FRANCE**, HE JOINED **NEWCASTLE** FROM **PARIS SAINT-GERMAIN** IN 1999, MOVING ON TO **FULHAM** TWO YEARS LATER. HE WON A FIRST DIVISION TITLE AND THE UEFA INTERTOTO CUP DURING HIS SIX SEASONS AT **CRAVEN COTTAGE**.

4 CAPPED 100 TIMES BY THE **REPUBLIC OF IRELAND**, HE WON THE LEAGUE CUP WITH **BLACKBURN**, TWO LEAGUE TITLES AND A LEAGUE CUP WITH **CHELSEA**, AND THE 2006 UEFA INTERTOTO CUP WITH **NEWCASTLE** BEFORE JOINING **FULHAM** IN 2009.

5 NOMADIC STRIKER AND MIDFIELDER WHO WON PROMOTIONS IN THE 1980S WITH **SHEFFIELD UNITED** AND **PRESTON NORTH END**. A BRIEF SPELL WITH **NEWCASTLE** ENDED IN RELEGATION AND HE JOINED **FULHAM** IN 1990, WHERE HE SPENT THE NEXT SIX SEASONS. IN HIS SUBSEQUENT COACHING CAREER HE SERVED AS CARETAKER MANAGER OF BOTH **NOTTS COUNTY** AND **NOTTINGHAM FOREST** ON NUMEROUS OCCASIONS.

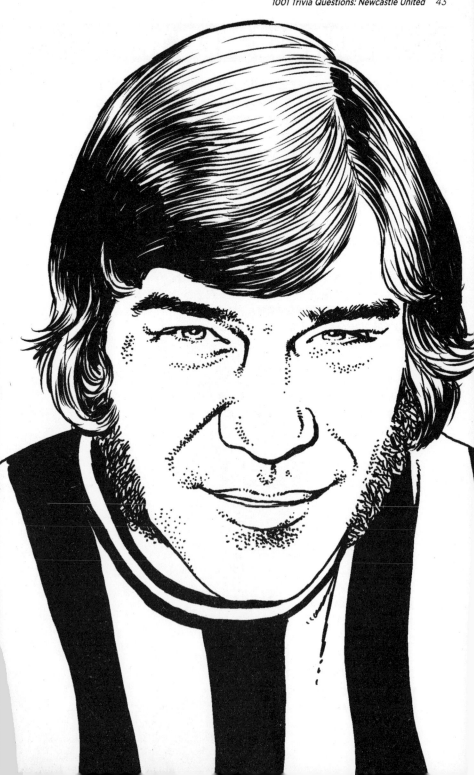

GEORDIE RED MEN

WHEN **LUIS SUÁREZ** JOINED **LIVERPOOL** FROM **AJAX** ON TRANSFER DEADLINE DAY IN 2011, THE £22.8 MILLION FEE MADE HIM THE MOST EXPENSIVE SIGNING IN THE **ANFIELD** CLUB'S HISTORY. HE ONLY HELD THE RECORD BRIEFLY -- HOURS LATER, **ANDY CARROLL** BECAME THE MOST EXPENSIVE BRITISH FOOTBALLER OF ALL TIME TO THAT POINT WHEN HE ARRIVED FROM **NEWCASTLE** IN A £35 MILLION DEAL.

IDENTIFY THESE OTHERS WHO HAVE PLAYED FOR BOTH **NEWCASTLE** AND **LIVERPOOL**:

1 HAVING WON HONOURS WITH **FEYENOORD** AND **PSV**, **NETHERLANDS** INTERNATIONAL WHO SPENT THE 2015-16 SEASON WITH **NEWCASTLE** BEFORE JOINING **LIVERPOOL**, WITH WHOM HE WON THE UEFA CHAMPIONS LEAGUE, THE PREMIER LEAGUE AND MORE. HE JOINED **PARIS SAINT-GERMAIN** IN THE SUMMER OF 2021.

2 JAMAICA-BORN WINGER WHO PLAYED 79 TIMES FOR **ENGLAND**.

3   SPANISH LEFT-BACK SIGNED FROM *VILLARREAL* IN 2007. HE WON A CHAMPIONSHIP WITH *NEWCASTLE* BEFORE SIGNING FOR *LIVERPOOL* IN A £7 MILLION DEAL IN 2011. HE ENDED HIS CAREER AT *REAL ZARAGOZA*, RETIRING IN 2017.

4   *LIVERPOOL* YOUTH PRODUCT WHO SPENT TIME ON LOAN AT *SOUTHAMPTON* AND *BOLTON WANDERERS* BEFORE JOINING *NEWCASTLE* IN 2008. A CHAMPIONSHIP WINNER, HE MOVED ON TO *READING*, *FULHAM* AND *BLACKBURN ROVERS*, SPENT TIME IN INDONESIAN FOOTBALL, PLAYED FOR *WALSALL* AND SIGNED FOR ICELAND'S *FRAM* IN 2021.

BAND OF MERRY MEN

BORN IN DERBY IN 1993, SON OF A PROFESSIONAL BASKETBALL PLAYER WITH THE *DERBY TRAILBLAZERS*, *JAMAAL LASCELLES* CAME THROUGH THE YOUTH SYSTEM AT *NOTTINGHAM FOREST*. HE JOINED *NEWCASTLE* IN THE SUMMER OF 2014 BUT WAS LOANED BACK TO *FOREST* FOR THE 2014-15 SEASON. HE WAS NAMED TEAM CAPTAIN AT THE END OF HIS FIRST SEASON PLAYING FOR *NEWCASTLE*.

NAME THESE OTHERS WHO PLAYED FOR *NOTTINGHAM FOREST:*

1 LOCAL LAD WHO WAS WITH *NEWCASTLE* FROM THE AGE OF 10 INTO HIS EARLY 20S. HE THRIVED AT *CARDIFF CITY*, PLAYED FOR *SUNDERLAND, IPSWICH TOWN, BLACKPOOL* AND MORE AND RETIRED IN 2016 AFTER PLAYING IN INDIAN SOCCER.

2 FULL-BACK WHO PLAYED MORE THAN 400 GAMES FOR *NEWCASTLE* BEFORE JOINING *FOREST*, WITH WHOM HE WON THE 1979 EUROPEAN CUP, THE FA CUP AND TWO LEAGUE CUPS. HE WENT ON TO MANAGE *FOREST* AND WAS LATER NAMED CLUB CHAIRMAN.

3 MIDFIELDER WHO PLAYED FOR *"THE MAGPIES"* IN THE MID-1980S. HE PLAYED FOR AND SUBSEQUENTLY MANAGED *NORWICH CITY, WEST BROMWICH ALBION, NOTTINGHAM FOREST* AND *SHEFFIELD WEDNESDAY*.

4 CAPPED 21 TIMES BY *ENGLAND*, MIDFIELDER WHO JOINED *NEWCASTLE* FROM *FOREST* IN 2002. HE SUBSEQUENTLY WON HONOURS WITH *TOTTENHAM HOTSPUR* AND *QPR*, BUT HIS CAREER WAS HAMPERED AND ULTIMATELY CURTAILED BY INJURIES.

5 DEFENDER WHO MADE OVER 200 APPEARANCES FOR *FOREST* BEFORE SIGNING FOR *NEWCASTLE* IN 2010 -- WHERE HE BECAME THE FIRST PLAYER TO RECEIVE FIVE YELLOW CARDS IN HIS FIRST FIVE PREMIER LEAGUE GAMES. HE SUBSEQUENTLY JOINED *WIGAN ATHLETIC, QPR, SCUNTHORPE UNITED* AND *MANSFIELD TOWN*.

6 THE FIRST PLAYER SINCE *LIONEL PÉREZ* IN 1998 TO TRANSFER DIRECTLY FROM *SUNDERLAND* TO NEWCASTLE, HE JOINED *FOREST* IN 2020 HAVING SPENT TIME ON LOAN AT THE CLUB.

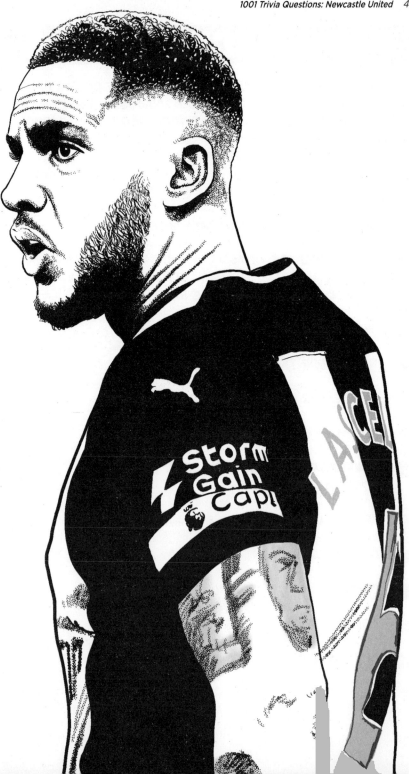

PAPERBACK WRITERS

THERE HAVE BEEN THREE *PAUL GASCOIGNE* AUTOBIOGRAPHIES TO DATE: *"GAZZA: MY STORY"* PUBLISHED IN 2004; *"BEING GAZZA: MY JOURNEY TO HELL AND BACK"* (WITH *HUNTER DAVIES* AND *JOHN MCKEOWN*), PUBLISHED IN 2006; AND *"GLORIOUS: MY WORLD, FOOTBALL AND ME"*, PUBLISHED IN 2011.

WHO WROTE THE FOLLOWING AUTOBIOGRAPHIES?

1   *"HOW NOT TO BE A FOOTBALL MILLIONAIRE"* -- 2013

2   *"NO NONSENSE"* -- 2016

3   *"OLD TOO SOON, SMART TOO LATE"* -- 2018

4   *"ANY GIVEN SATURDAY"* -- 2017

5   *"LIVING FOR THE MOMENT"* -- 2017

6   *"A GREATER GLORY: FROM PITCH TO PULPIT"* -- 2021

7   *"CLOWN PRINCE OF SOCCER"* -- 1955

8   *"FAST FORWARD: THE HARD ROAD TO FOOTBALL SUCCESS"* -- 2020

9   *"FOOTBALL: MY LIFE, MY PASSION"* -- 2017

10   *"FAREWELL BUT NOT GOODBYE"* -- 2005

11   *"REBOOT: MY LIFE"* -- 2019

12   *"SIR LES"* -- 1997

13   *"TO CAP IT ALL"* -- 2009

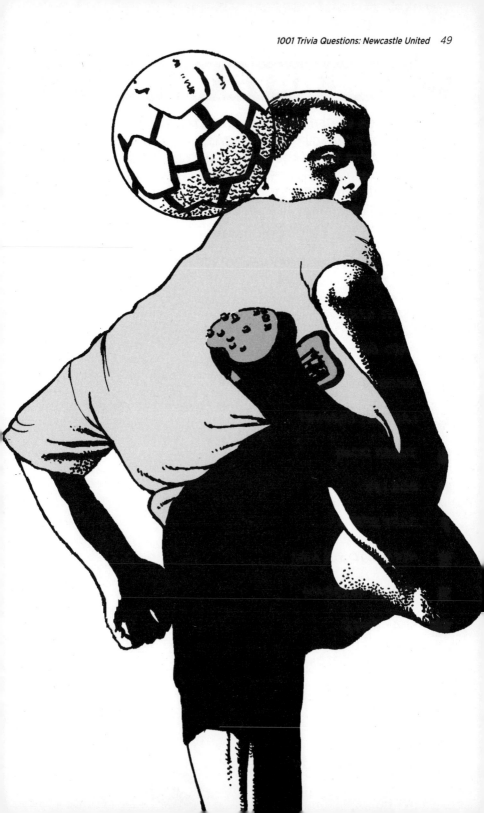

THE BOYS OF '99

CAPPED 59 TIMES BY *GERMANY* -- HE WAS A MEMBER OF THE SIDE THAT LOST THE 2002 WORLD CUP FINAL TO *BRAZIL* -- *DIETMAR HAMANN* WON THE UEFA CUP, TWO LEAGUE TITLES AND TWO DOMESTIC CUPS WITH *BAYERN MUNICH* AND THE UEFA CHAMPIONS LEAGUE, UEFA CUP, TWO FA CUPS AND MORE WITH *LIVERPOOL*. IN BETWEEN, HE SPENT ONE SEASON ON TYNESIDE, DURING WHICH HE PLAYED IN THE 1999 FA CUP FINAL 2-0 LOSS TO *MANCHESTER UNITED*.

WHICH CLUB DID THE FOLLOWING MEMBERS OF THE 1999 FA CUP FINAL TEAM JOIN NEXT?

1   *STEVE HARPER*

2   *ANDY GRIFFIN*

3   *NIKOS DABIZAS*

4   *LAURENT CHARVET*

5   *DIDIER DOMI*

6   *ROB LEE*

7   *GARY SPEED*

8   *NOLBERTO SOLANO*

9   *TEMUR KETSBAIA*

10 *SHAY GIVEN*

11 *WARREN BARTON*

12 *SILVIO MARIĆ*

13 *STEPHEN GLASS*

14 *DUNCAN FERGUSON*

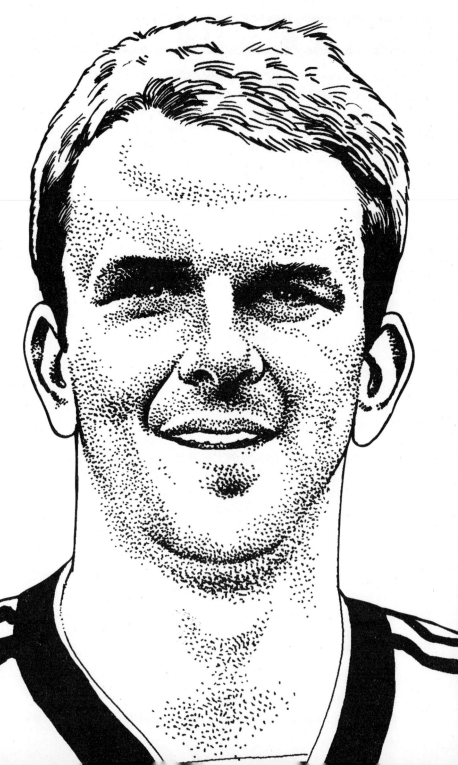

BLACK & WHITE CHERRIES

A £3 MILLION SIGNING FROM *COVENTRY CITY* IN 2014, STRIKER *CALLUM WILSON* SCORED 20 GOALS IN HIS DEBUT SEASON WITH *BOURNEMOUTH* TO HELP *"THE CHERRIES"* ACHIEVE PROMOTION TO THE PREMIER LEAGUE FOR THE FIRST TIME IN THE CLUB'S HISTORY. DURING HIS SIX YEARS AT THE CLUB, HE BECAME THE FIRST *BOURNEMOUTH* PLAYER TO SCORE FOR *ENGLAND.* HE JOINED *NEWCASTLE* IN 2020 FOR A FEE BELIEVED TO BE IN THE REGION OF £20 MILLION.

IDENTIFY THESE OTHERS WHO HAVE PLAYED FOR *BOURNEMOUTH* AND *NEWCASTLE UNITED:*

1 HAVING LEARNED HIS TRADE AT *QPR, GILLINGHAM* AND *BOURNEMOUTH,* HE JOINED *NEWCASTLE UNITED* IN 1990, WHERE HIS GOALS HELPED FIRE *"THE MAGPIES"* TO PROMOTION TO THE TOP FLIGHT IN 1993. HE WENT ON TO PLAY FOR *CHELSEA* BEFORE RETURNING TO *QPR,* WHERE HE RETIRED IN 2002.

2 *SCOTLAND* INTERNATIONAL WINGER WHO WON PROMOTIONS WITH *SWINDON TOWN* AND *BOURNEMOUTH* BEFORE JOINING *NEWCASTLE* IN 2016, WITH WHOM HE WON PROMOTION TO THE PREMIER LEAGUE IN HIS DEBUT SEASON.

3 MIDFIELDER WHO PLAYED FOR *PLYMOUTH ARGYLE, EVERTON* AND *NEWCASTLE* BEFORE JOINING *BOURNEMOUTH* IN 2014. HAVING SPENT SIX-AND-A-HALF YEARS WITH *"THE CHERRIES",* DURING WHICH TIME THE CLUB WAS PROMOTED TO THE PREMIER LEAGUE, HE JOINED *WATFORD* IN EARLY 2021.

4 *SCOTLAND* WINGER WHO LEFT *BOURNEMOUTH* FOR *NEWCASTLE* IN 2020 HAVING LET HIS CONTRACT RUN DOWN.

5 HAVING PLAYED FOR A NUMBER OF CLUBS, INCLUDING *NEWCASTLE, BOURNEMOUTH, CRYSTAL PALACE, IPSWICH TOWN* AND *WATFORD,* HE WORKED UNDER *BOBBY ROBSON* AS A COACH AT *IPSWICH,* AND SCOUT AT *ENGLAND* AND *NEWCASTLE.*

6 *NORTHERN IRELAND* RIGHT-BACK WHO PLAYED MORE THAN 200 GAMES FOR *NEWCASTLE* BEFORE JOINING *BOURNEMOUTH* IN 1964.

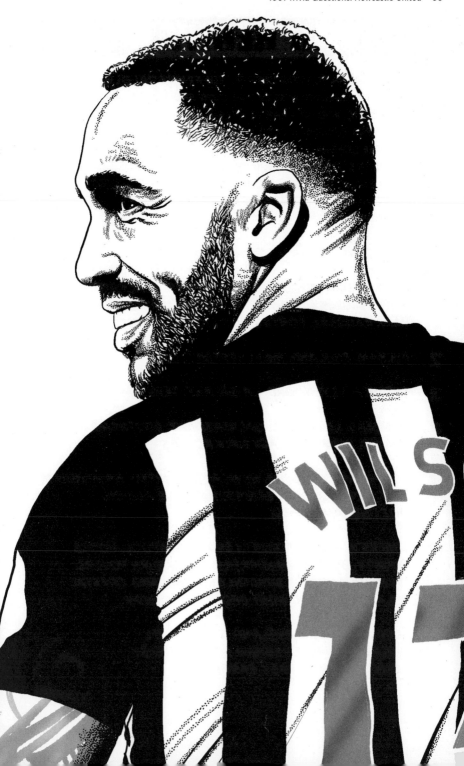

SIR KENNY D

DURING HIS STELLAR PLAYING CAREER, **SIR KENNY DALGLISH** WON FOUR LEAGUE TITLES, FOUR SCOTTISH CUPS AND A SCOTTISH LEAGUE CUP WITH **CELTIC**, AND SIX LEAGUE TITLES, THE FA CUP, FOUR LEAGUE CUPS AND THREE EUROPEAN CUPS WITH **LIVERPOOL**. AS A MANAGER, HE WON THREE LEAGUE TITLES AND THREE DOMESTIC CUPS WITH **LIVERPOOL**, A SCOTTISH LEAGUE CUP WITH **CELTIC**, PROMOTION AND A PREMIER LEAGUE TITLE WITH **BLACKBURN ROVERS**. UNFORTUNATELY, HIS 20 MONTHS AT THE HELM OF **NEWCASTLE** FAILED TO BRING SILVERWARE.

WHICH **NEWCASTLE** BOSS ALSO MANAGED:

1 **BOSTON UNITED, COLCHESTER UNITED, BLACKBURN ROVERS, BIRMINGHAM CITY, OXFORD UNITED, QUEENS PARK RANGERS, PORTSMOUTH, DERBY COUNTY**

2 **FULHAM, ENGLAND, MANCHESTER CITY**

3 **CHELSEA, FEYENOORD, LA GALAXY, TEREK GROZNY**

4 **RANGERS, LIVERPOOL, GALATASARAY, SOUTHAMPTON, TORINO, BENFICA, BLACKBURN ROVERS**

5 **TOTTENHAM HOTSPUR, NEWCASTLE UNITED, BIRMINGHAM CITY, NORWICH CITY, BRIGHTON & HOVE ALBION, NOTTINGHAM FOREST**

6 **LIMERICK, PRESTON NORTH END, BLACKPOOL, NOTTS COUNTY, BOLTON WANDERERS, BLACKBURN ROVERS, WEST HAM UNITED, SUNDERLAND, ENGLAND, CRYSTAL PALACE, EVERTON, WEST BROMWICH ALBION**

7 **MIDDLESBROUGH, ENGLAND, TWENTE, VFL WOLFSBURG, NOTTINGHAM FOREST, DERBY COUNTY, QUEENS PARK RANGERS**

8 *REAL MADRID U17, REAL MADRID CASTILLA, VALLADOLID, OSASUNA, EXTREMADURA, TENERIFE, VALENCIA, LIVERPOOL, INTERNAZIONALE, CHELSEA, NAPOLI, REAL MADRID, DALIAN PROFESSIONAL, EVERTON*

9 *BOURNEMOUTH, BURNLEY*

CHAMPIONS OF EUROPE

HAVING WON THE UEFA CHAMPIONS LEAGUE, TWO LEAGUE TITLES AND MORE WITH **AJAX** AND LA LIGA WITH **BARCELONA**, DUTCH SUPERSTAR **PATRICK KLUIVERT** JOINED **NEWCASTLE** ON A FREE TRANSFER IN 2004. HE WENT ON TO PLAY FOR **VALENCIA**, **PSV** AND **LILLE** BEFORE EMBARKING ON A COACHING AND MANAGEMENT CAREER AT THE HIGHEST LEVELS OF CLUB AND INTERNATIONAL FOOTBALL.

WITH WHICH TEAMS DID THESE **NEWCASTLE** PLAYERS WIN A UEFA EUROPEAN CUP OR CHAMPIONS LEAGUE?

1 *DAVIDE SANTON*

2 *JAMES MILNER*

3 *LOUIS SAHA*

4 *TERRY MCDERMOTT*

5 *JOHN DAHL TOMASSON*

6 *NICKY BUTT*

7 *FRANK CLARK*

8 *KEVIN KEEGAN*

9 *DIETMAR HAMANN*

10 *ANDY COLE*

11 *RONNY JOHNSEN*

12 *GEREMI*

13 *GEORGINIO WIJNALDUM*

14 *PETER WITHE*

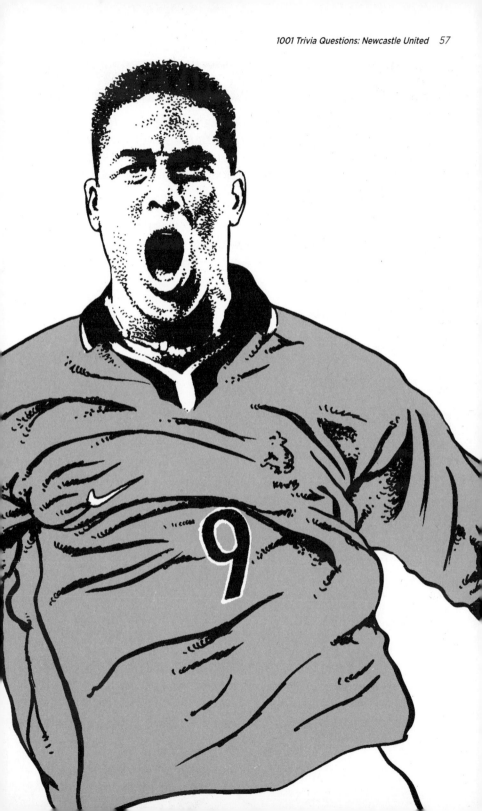

BRUCE BUYS

HAVING JOINED **ARSENAL** WHEN HE WAS FOUR YEARS OLD, **JOE WILLOCK** MADE HIS HIS PREMIER LEAGUE DEBUT AGAINST **NEWCASTLE UNITED** IN 2018 AT THE AGE OF 18. HE JOINED **"THE MAGPIES"** ON LOAN IN EARLY 2021, THE DEAL BEING MADE PERMANENT THAT SUMMER, FOR A FEE REPORTED TO BE £25 MILLION.

WILLOCK WAS A **STEVE BRUCE** SIGNING. FROM WHICH CLUBS WERE THE FOLLOWING PLAYERS SIGNED DURING **BRUCE'S** TENURE?

1 JOELINTON

2 ALLAN SAINT-MAXIMIN

3 DANNY ROSE

4 NABIL BENTALEB

5 ANDY CARROLL

6 EMIL KRAFTH

7 JETRO WILLEMS

8 JAMAL LEWIS

9 MARK GILLESPIE

10 JEFF HENDRICK

11 JAKE TURNER

12 VALENTINO LAZARO

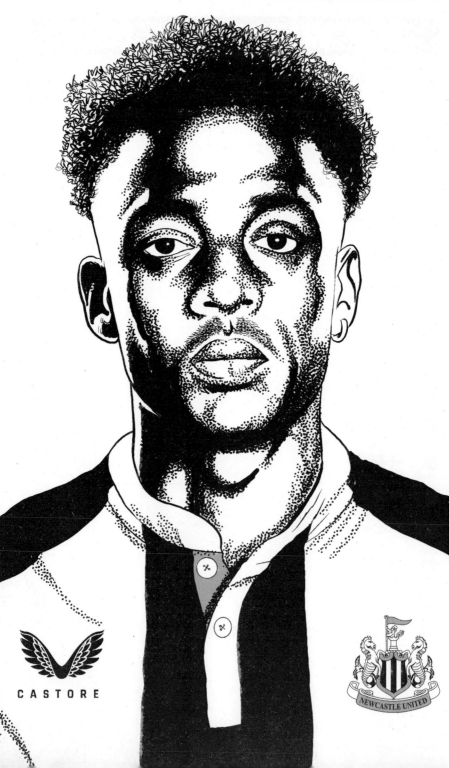

THE WIZARD OF NOD

EARLY IN HIS STELLAR CAREER, STRIKER **PETER WITHE** SPENT A SEASON IN THE NORTH AMERICAN SOCCER LEAGUE WITH **PORTLAND TIMBERS**, RACKING UP 17 GOALS AND 7 ASSISTS IN 22 GAMES TO HELP WIN THE TITLE. HIS AERIAL PROWESS EARNED HIM THE NICKNAMES **"THE MAD HEADER"** AND **"THE WIZARD OF NOD"**.

IDENTIFY THE **NEWCASTLE** PLAYER BY HIS NICKNAME:

1 *THE LEAP*

2 *THE CLOWN PRINCE*

3 *ONE SIZE*

4 *NED*

5 *SARGE*

6 *PEDRO*

7 *SALTY*

8 *DAZZLER*

9 *ZICO*

10 *PSYCHO*

11 *THE GOOCH*

12 *SPIDERMAN*

13 *THE GALLOPING CHIP* OR *BAMBER*

14 *CASSIUS*

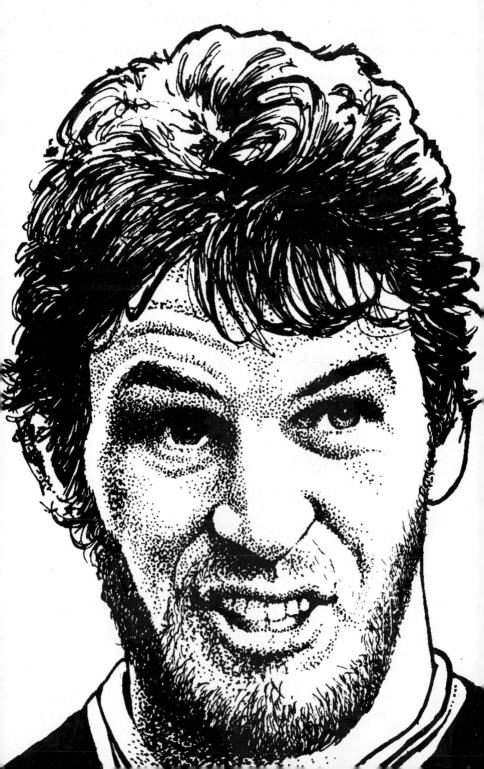

TOFFEEMEN

IN A CAREER THAT EARNED HIM 59 *ENGLAND* CAPS, *PETER BEARDSLEY* BECAME ONE OF THE SELECT BAND WHO HAVE PLAYED FOR BOTH *EVERTON* AND *LIVERPOOL*. HE ALSO PLAYED FOR *CARLISLE UNITED, NEWCASTLE, BOLTON WANDERERS, MANCHESTER CITY, FULHAM, HARTLEPOOL UNITED* AND TEAMS IN CANADA AND AUSTRALIA.

IDENTIFY THESE OTHERS WHO PLAYED FOR BOTH *NEWCASTLE* AND *EVERTON*:

1   *SCOTLAND* STRIKER WHO SPENT TWO INJURY-HAMPERED SEASONS ON TYNESIDE FROM 1998 TO 2000, IN BETWEEN TWO LENGTHY SPELLS WITH *EVERTON*, THE CLUB WHERE HE SUBSEQUENTLY BEGAN HIS COACHING CAREER.

2 CENTRE-HALF WHO PLAYED FOR BOTH CLUBS BEFORE WINNING THE 1966 SECOND DIVISION TITLE, THE 1968 LEAGUE CHAMPIONSHIP, 1969 LEAGUE CUP AND THE EUROPEAN CUP WINNERS' CUP WITH *MANCHESTER CITY.*

3 ITALIAN FULL-BACK SIGNED TO *NEWCASTLE* FROM *INTER* IN 1997, HE JOINED *EVERTON* THREE YEARS LATER BUT HIS SEVEN SEASONS ON MERSEYSIDE WERE RAVAGED BY INJURIES.

4 FRENCH CENTRAL DEFENDER WHO JOINED *NEWCASTLE* ON LOAN FROM *PSG* IN THE EARLY 2000S, BEFORE PLAYING FOR *MANCHESTER CITY, PORTSMOUTH, EVERTON* AND *BOURNEMOUTH.* HE PLAYED FIFTEEN CONSECUTIVE SEASONS IN THE PREMIER LEAGUE, MAKING 450 APPEARANCES.

5 HAVING PLAYED IN THE 2009 FA CUP FINAL WITH *EVERTON,* MIDFIELDER WHO FAILED TO MAKE AN IMPACT IN HIS TWO SEASONS AT *NEWCASTLE,* BUT WENT ON TO SPEND SIX-AND-A-HALF SUCCESSFUL YEARS AT *BOURNEMOUTH,* WINNING PROMOTION TO THE TOP FLIGHT IN 2015. HE JOINED *WATFORD* IN 2021.

6 THE YOUNGEST PERSON EVER TO PLAY FOR *NEWCASTLE* WHEN HE MADE HIS DEBUT IN 1990, ALL-ROUNDER WHO LEFT FOR *ASTON VILLA* AFTER THE 1998 FA CUP FINAL. HE WENT ON TO PLAY FOR *EVERTON, WEST BROM* AND *SHEFFIELD WEDNESDAY* BEFORE EMBARKING ON A COACHING AND MANAGEMENT CAREER.

7 CAPPED THREE TIMES BY *ENGLAND,* HIS PLAYING CAREER TOOK HIM FROM *STOKE CITY* TO *EVERTON, NEWCASTLE* AND *FULHAM,* WITH THREE SEPARATE SPELLS AT *SUNDERLAND.*

8 *REPUBLIC OF IRELAND* MIDFIELDER WHO LEFT *LIVERPOOL* FOR *EVERTON* AS A LEAGUE CUP WINNER IN 1982. HE WON TWO LEAGUE TITLES AND THE EUROPEAN CUP WINNERS' CUP IN HIS TEN YEARS AT *GOODISON,* BEFORE MOVING ON TO *NEWCASTLE,* WHERE HE ADDED A CHAMPIONSHIP MEDAL TO HIS HAUL.

9 NOMADIC FORWARD WHOSE NICKNAME INSPIRED AN INFLATABLE BANANA CRAZE AMONG *MANCHESTER CITY* FANS IN THE LATE 1980S.

GOALGETTER GREATS

ALAN SHEARER SCORED A RECORD 206 GOALS FOR **NEWCASTLE**, TOPPING THE CLUB'S GOALSCORING CHARTS IN EACH OF THE TEN SEASONS IN WHICH HE PARTICIPATED (ALBEIT TIED WITH OTHER PLAYERS IN TWO OF THOSE SEASONS).

IDENTIFY THESE OTHER **NEWCASTLE** GOALGETTER GREATS:

1 200 GOALS (1943-1957): **ENGLAND** INTERNATIONAL WHO WENT ON TO PLAY FOR **LINFIELD**, HE WAS KNOWN AS **"WOR JACKIE"**

2 153 GOALS (1953-1962): CENTRE-FORWARD WHO WENT ON TO PLAY FOR **HUDDERSFIELD TOWN**

3 143 GOALS (1925-1930): SCORED 24 GOALS IN 20 GAMES FOR **SCOTLAND**

4 121 GOALS (1971-1976): **SUPERMAC**

5 119 GOALS (1983-1997): CAPPED 59 TIMES FOR **ENGLAND**, HE PLAYED FOR BOTH MANCHESTER AND BOTH LIVERPOOL CLUBS

6 113 GOALS (1921-1931): SCOTTISH INSIDE-FORWARD WHO WON LEAGUE AND CUP HONOURS IN HIS TIME ON TYNESIDE

7 113 GOALS (1949-1961): HE WON THREE FA CUPS IN FIVE YEARS

8 101 GOALS (1920-1925): HE SCORED THE FIRST GOAL IN THE 1924 FA CUP FINAL VICTORY

9 97 GOALS (1962-1971): AFTER LEAVING **NEWCASTLE** HE YO-YOED BETWEEN **WEST HAM, SUNDERLAND** AND **CARLISLE UNITED** AS WELL AS PLAYING FOR **CHELSEA** AND **GATESHEAD**

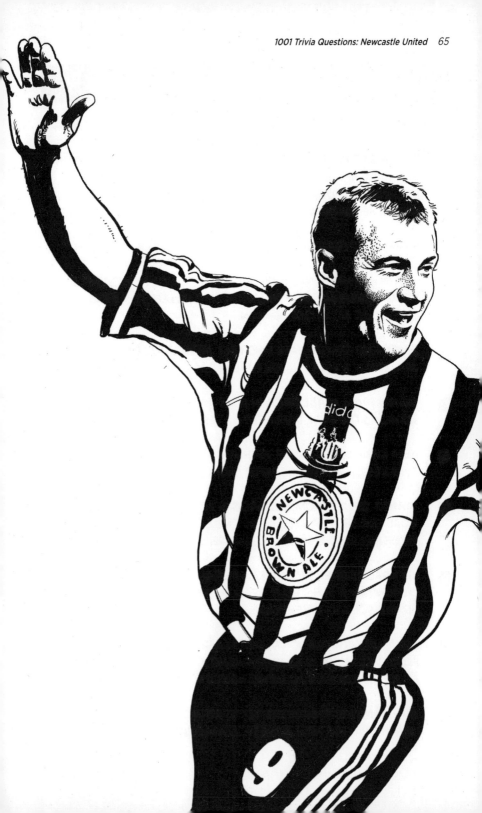

THE SPAIN DRAIN

MICHAEL OWEN JOINED NEWCASTLE FROM REAL MADRID IN A £16.8 MILLION DEAL IN 2005. THE ENGLAND STRIKER HAD SCORED 13 GOALS FOR "LOS MERENGUES" IN HIS YEAR AT THE BERNABÉU. FOLLOWING A BRIGHT START, HIS TIME WITH "THE MAGPIES" WAS DERAILED BY INJURIES. WHEN HIS FOURTH SEASON WITH NEWCASTLE CULMINATED IN RELEGATION, HE JOINED MANCHESTER UNITED ON A FREE TRANSFER.

IDENTIFY THESE OTHERS WHO PLAYED IN SPANISH FOOTBALL:

1 SPAIN INTERNATIONAL MIDFIELDER WHO JOINED NEWCASTLE FROM BORUSSIA DORTMUND IN 2017, HE LEFT FOR REAL SOCIEDAD AFTER ONE SEASON.

2 ENGLAND CENTRE-BACK WHO LEFT NEWCASTLE FOR REAL MADRID IN A £13.4 MILLION DEAL IN 2004.

3 SIGNED FROM MALLORCA IN 2008, HIS SEVEN SEASONS AT NEWCASTLE WERE DISRUPTED BY TESTICULAR CANCER.

4 UEFA CHAMPIONS LEAGUE WINNER WITH AJAX, HE ARRIVED ON TYNESIDE ON A FREE TRANSFER FROM BARCELONA IN 2004.

5 STRIKER SIGNED FROM MONACO IN 2014, HE SCORED ONE LEAGUE GOAL FOR NEWCASTLE IN HIS TWO SEASONS AT THE CLUB -- WHICH INCLUDED A BARREN LOAN SPELL IN SPAIN WITH OSASUNA.

6 LEFT-BACK SIGNED FROM VILLARREAL IN 2007, HE WON A LEAGUE CHAMPIONSHIP IN HIS FOUR SEASONS WITH NEWCASTLE BEFORE HE WAS SOLD TO LIVERPOOL.

7 URUGUAY INTERNATIONAL MIDFIELDER WHOSE LOAN SIGNING FROM VALENCIA IN 2008 APPARENTLY SPARKED THE RESIGNATION OF KEVIN KEEGAN AS NEWCASTLE MANAGER IN PROTEST!

8 ENGLAND RIGHT-BACK SIGNED TO NEWCASTLE IN 2022 AFTER WINNING LA LIGA WITH ATLÉTICO MADRID.

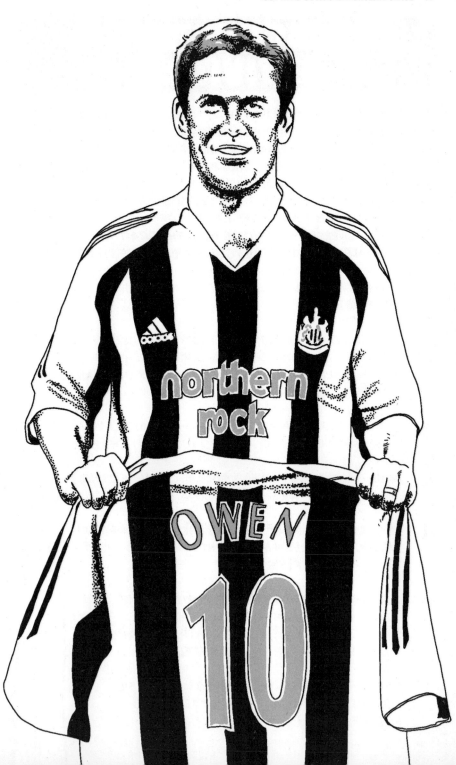

EXTRACURRICULAR ACTIVITIES

DAVID GINOLA'S EXTRACURRICULAR ACTIVITIES INCLUDED CATWALK MODELLING AND PRODUCT ENDORSEMENTS FOR EVERYTHING FROM *RENAULT* CARS TO HAIR PRODUCTS. HAVING ATTENDED ACTING CLASSES AT *RADA,* HE MADE HIS SCREEN DEBUT PLAYING *DIDIER THE BUTCHER,* A LEADING ROLE IN THE ANGLO-FRENCH SHORT FILM *"ROSBEEF".* SUBSEQUENT CREDITS INCLUDED THE ROLE OF GERMAN SNIPER *CORPORAL DIETER MAX* IN *"THE LAST DROP"* AND APPEARANCES ON SHOWS AS DIVERSE AS *"AT HOME WITH THE BRAITHWAITES"* AND THE AMERICAN SOAP OPERA *"THE YOUNG AND THE RESTLESS".*

1 WHICH *NEWCASTLE* STAR FRONTED A SALSA BAND CALLED *THE GEORDIE LATINOS* ?

2 WHICH *NEWCASTLE, QPR* AND *CRYSTAL PALACE* DEFENDER APPEARED AS A YOUNGSTER IN THE OPENING SCENES OF THE 1997 *BRUCE WILLIS, MILLA JOVOVICH* AND *GARY OLDMAN* MOVIE *"THE FIFTH ELEMENT"* ?

3 ON WHICH 2000 SIX-PART TV SERIES DID *MICHAEL OWEN* STAR AS HIMSELF GIVING REGULAR ADVICE TO YOUNG BOY *CHARLIE?*

4 *PAUL GASCOIGNE* EARNED A GOLD DISC WITH HIS UK NO. 2 HIT *"FOG ON THE TYNE"* -- A COLLABORATION WITH WHICH GROUP?

5 WHAT WAS THE NAME OF THE POP SINGLE THAT TOOK *CHRIS WADDLE* AND *GLENN HODDLE* INTO THE TOP 20 AND ON TO *"TOP OF THE POPS"* IN 1987?

6 DURING HIS TIME AT *MARSEILLE, CHRIS WADDLE* TEAMED UP WITH WHICH *FRANCE* DEFENDER -- SUBSEQUENTLY A LEAGUE TITLE WINNER WITH *RANGERS* -- ON THE SINGLE *"WE'VE GOT A FEELING"* ?

7 ON WHICH ACCLAIMED 1982 TV SERIES DID *GRAEME SOUNESS* INTERACT WITH A CHARACTER CALLED *YOSSER HUGHES* ?

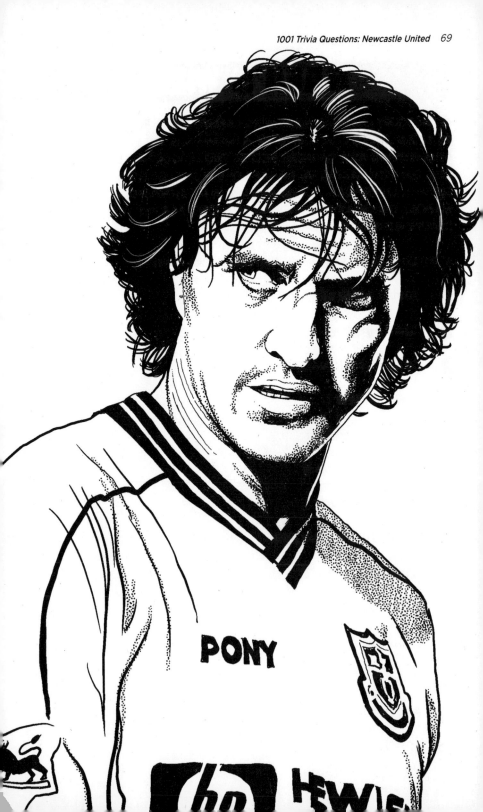

RAFA'S MEN

AFTER INJURY CURTAILED HIS PLAYING CAREER, **RAFA BENITEZ** JOINED **REAL MADRID'S** COACHING STAFF IN HIS MID-20S. HIS SUBSEQUENT ACHIEVEMENTS AS A MANAGER INCLUDE TWO LEAGUE TITLES AND THE UEFA CUP WITH **VALENCIA**, THE UEFA CHAMPIONS LEAGUE AND FA CUP WITH **LIVERPOOL**, CUP HONOURS WITH **INTERNAZIONALE** AND **NAPOLI**, THE UEFA EUROPA LEAGUE WITH **CHELSEA** AND THE 2017 CHAMPIONSHIP WITH **NEWCASTLE**.

AT WHICH CLUB DID HE MANAGE THE FOLLOWING PLAYERS:

1 *JAVIER MASCHERANO*

2 *JUAN MATA*

3 *CRISTIANO RONALDO*

4 *JOHN CAREW*

5 *WESLEY SNEIJDER*

6 *GONZALO HIGUAÍN*

7 *ASMIR BEGOVIĆ*

8 *GEORGINIO WIJNALDUM*

9 *YANNICK CARASCO*

10 *NATHAN AKÉ*

11 *EDEN HAZARD*

12 *PHILIPPE COUTINHO*

13 *AYOZE PÉREZ*

14 *JORGINHO*

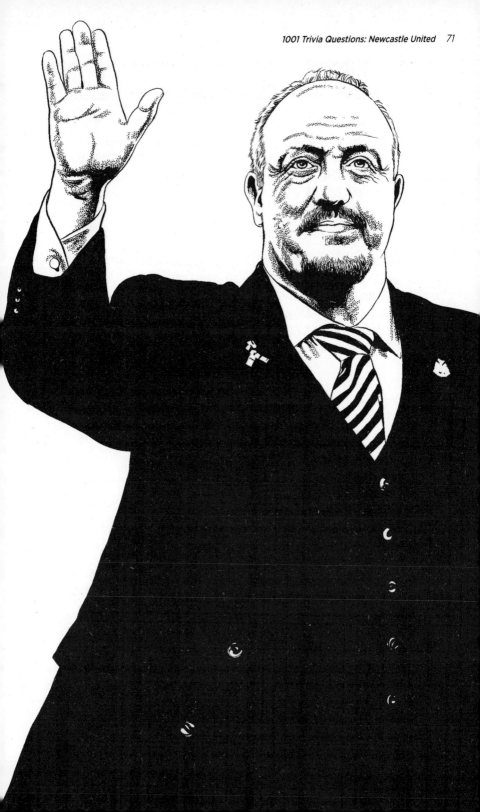

RED DEVIL MAGPIES

HAVING WON A UEFA CHAMPIONS LEAGUE, SIX PREMIER LEAGUE TITLES, THREE FA CUPS AND MORE WITH **MANCHESTER UNITED**, **ENGLAND** MIDFIELDER **NICKY BUTT** JOINED **NEWCASTLE UNITED** IN 2004. HE SPENT SIX SEASONS ON TYNESIDE, DURING WHICH TIME HE WON A LEAGUE CHAMPIONSHIP AND THE UEFA INTERTOTO CUP.

IDENTIFY THE FOLLOWING WHO PLAYED FOR BOTH **UNITEDS** :

1 **FRANCE** STRIKER WHO SPENT TIME ON LOAN FROM **METZ** AT **NEWCASTLE** EARLY IN HIS CAREER, WON PROMOTION WITH **FULHAM**, TWO PREMIER LEAGUE TITLES, THE LEAGUE CUP AND THE 2008 UEFA CHAMPIONS LEAGUE WITH **MANCHESTER UNITED** AND WENT ON TO PLAY FOR **EVERTON**, **TOTTENHAM HOTSPUR**, **SUNDERLAND** AND **LAZIO**.

2 WINGER CAPPED 86 TIMES BY **NORTHERN IRELAND**, HE JOINED **NEWCASTLE** FROM **MANCHESTER UNITED** IN 1995, BEFORE GOING ON TO WIN THE LEAGUE CUP WITH **BLACKBURN ROVERS**, PLAY FOR **WIGAN ATHLETIC**, **LEICESTER CITY**, **SHEFFIELD UNITED** AND MORE AND WIN AN IRISH LEAGUE CUP WITH **GLENTORAN** IN 2010.

3 **ITALY** INTERNATIONAL BORN IN THE UNITED STATES, HE SPENT TIME ON LOAN AT **NEWCASTLE** FROM **MANCHESTER UNITED** IN 2006 BEFORE GOING ON TO PLAY FOR **VILLARREAL**.

4 ONE OF THE **"BUSBY BABES"** WHO SURVIVED THE 1958 MUNICH AIR DISASTER, HE WENT ON TO PLAY FOR **NEWCASTLE**, **LINCOLN CITY** AND **MANSFIELD TOWN**.

5 **ENGLAND** STRIKER WHOSE RECORD-BREAKING TRANSFER FROM **NEWCASTLE** TO **MANCHESTER UNITED** IN 1995 SPARKED PROTESTS AND A PUBLIC CONFRONTATION BETWEEN MANAGER **KEVIN KEEGAN** AND FANS AT **ST JAMES' PARK**.

6 FRENCH WINGER WHO LEFT **MANCHESTER UNITED** FOR **NEWCASTLE** IN 2011, WHERE HE SPENT FIVE SEASONS BEFORE GOING ON TO PLAY IN RUSSIA, TURKEY, BULGARIA AND THE USA.

7 HAVING JOINED *MANCHESTER UNITED* IN 2004 FOLLOWING RELEGATION WITH *LEEDS UNITED*, HE JOINED *NEWCASTLE* IN 2007. HE WENT ON TO PLAY FOR *MK DONS* AND *NOTTS COUNTY*.

8 *REPUBLIC OF IRELAND* MIDFIELDER WHO WON MULTIPLE HONOURS WITH *SHAMROCK ROVERS*, SPENT TWO YEARS AT *OLD TRAFFORD* AND THEN SIX YEARS WITH *NEWCASTLE*, WITH WHOM HE WON A FIRST DIVISION TITLE IN 1993.

THE CHINESE CONNECTION

NOMADIC *NIGERIA* INTERNATIONAL *OBAFEMI MARTINS* WON ITALIAN LEAGUE AND CUP HONOURS WITH *INTERNAZIONALE*, THE UEFA INTERTOTO CUP WITH *NEWCASTLE*, THE LEAGUE CUP WITH *BIRMINGHAM CITY*, RUSSIAN LEAGUE AND CUP HONOURS WITH *RUBIN KAZAN* AND TROPHIES WITH *SEATTLE SOUNDERS*. HAVING WON THE CHINESE FA CUP WITH *SHANGHAI SHENHUA*, HE SIGNED FOR *WUHAN ZALL* IN 2020.

IDENTIFY THESE OTHERS WITH CONNECTIONS TO *NEWCASTLE* AND CHINA:

1 FRENCH-BORN *SENEGAL* INTERNATIONAL STRIKER WHO PLAYED FOR *WEST HAM, NEWCASTLE* AND *CHELSEA*, CLUBS IN FRANCE, BELGIUM, TURKEY AND ITALY, AND HAD TWO SPELLS WITH *SHANGHAI SHENHUA*.

2 *ENGLAND* MIDFIELDER WHOSE CLUBS INCLUDE *NEWCASTLE, SPURS, LAZIO, RANGERS, MIDDLESBROUGH, EVERTON, BURNLEY* AND *GANSU TIANMA*.

3 *IVORY COAST* MIDFIELDER WHO WON HONOURS WITH *ANDERLECHT* AND *TWENTE* BEFORE JOINING *"THE MAGPIES"* IN 2010. HE SPENT SEVEN SEASONS ON TYNESIDE BEFORE JOINING *BEIJING ENTERPRISES GROUP*. FOUR MONTHS AFTER ARRIVING IN CHINA, THE 30-YEAR-OLD COLLAPSED AND DIED IN TRAINING.

4 *VENEZUELA* STAR VOTED *NEWCASTLE* PLAYER OF THE YEAR IN 2019 WHILE ON LOAN FROM *WEST BROM*, HE PLAYED IN SPAIN AND RUSSIA, SPENT 18 MONTHS IN CHINA WITH *DALIAN PROFESSIONAL* AND SIGNED FOR *EVERTON* IN 2021.

5 *SENEGAL* STRIKER WHOSE FOUR-AND-A-HALF SEASONS WITH NEWCASTLE BROUGHT 44 GOALS AND -- IN 2015 -- A SEVEN-MATCH BAN. HE LEFT FOR *SHANDONG LUNENG* IN 2016.

6 MANAGER WHO TOOK THE HELM AT *DALIAN PROFESSIONAL* AFTER LEAVING *NEWCASTLE* IN 2019.

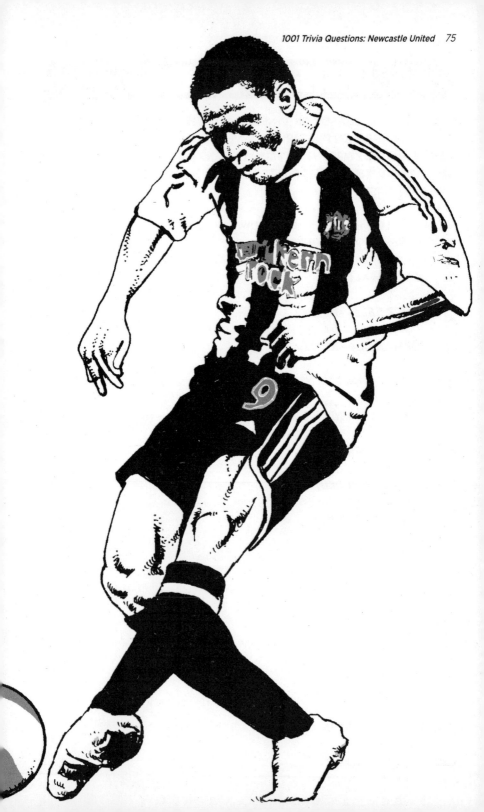

JONJO JOINS

IN HIS FIRST FULL SEASON ON TYNESIDE AFTER HIS £12 MILLION ARRIVAL FROM **SWANSEA CITY** IN EARLY 2016, **ENGLAND** MIDFIELDER **JONJO SHELVEY** MADE 46 APPEARANCES AND SCORED 5 GOALS AS **NEWCASTLE** WERE PROMOTED TO THE PREMIER LEAGUE AFTER WINNING THE CHAMPIONSHIP TITLE.

FROM WHICH CLUBS WERE THE FOLLOWING MEMBERS OF THE 2016-17 CHAMPIONSHIP SQUAD SIGNED?

1   KARL DARLOW

2   MATZ SELS

3   CIARAN CLARK

4   GRANT HANLEY

5   JAMAAL LASCELLES

6   CHANCEL MBEMBA

7   DEANDRE YEDLIN

8   JACK COLBACK

9   VURNON ANITA

10   MATT RITCHIE

11   ISAAC HAYDEN

12   MOHAMED DIAMÉ

13   YOAN GOUFFRAN

14   CHRISTIAN ATSU

15   DWIGHT GAYLE

16 *AYOZE PÉREZ*

17 *DARYL MURPHY*

18 *ALEKSANDAR MITROVIĆ*

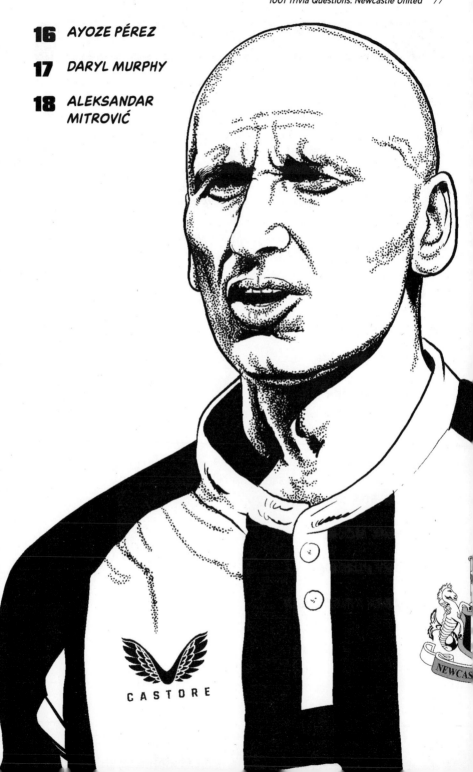

"BALD EAGLE" BUYS

AFTER EIGHT SEASONS AT *ARSENAL, ENGLAND* FULL-BACK *KENNY SANSOM* JOINED *NEWCASTLE* IN LATE 1988. ON HIS RETURN TO HIGHBURY WITH HIS NEW TEAM THE FOLLOWING APRIL, *SANSOM* SCORED AGAINST HIS OLD CLUB ... ONLY FOR THE GOAL TO BE DISALLOWED. *ARSENAL* WENT ON TO WIN THE GAME 1-0. HAD *SANSOM'S* GOAL BEEN ALLOWED TO STAND, *ARSENAL* MAY WELL HAVE MISSED OUT ON GLORY THAT SEASON. *"THE GUNNERS"* WON THE TITLE ON GOAL DIFFERENCE FROM *LIVERPOOL* ... WHILE *"THE MAGPIES"* WERE RELEGATED!

SANSOM WAS A *JIM SMITH* RECRUIT TO *NEWCASTLE* -- FROM WHICH CLUBS DID *"BALD EAGLE" SMITH* SIGN THE FOLLOWING?

1 *ROY AITKEN*

2 *MICKY QUINN*

3 *PAVEL SRNÍČEK*

4 *KEVIN BROCK*

5 *GARY BRAZIL*

6 *GAVIN PEACOCK*

7 *NEIL SIMPSON*

8 *MARK MCGHEE*

9 *JOHN BURRIDGE*

10 *BJØRN KRISTENSEN*

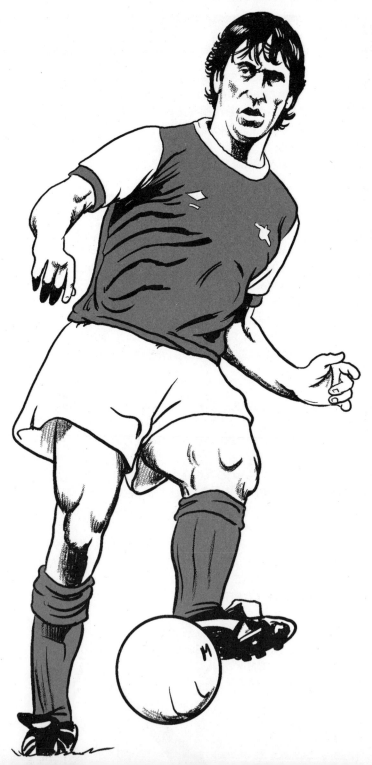

MAKING AN ENTRANCE

FOLLOWING HIS £13,000 SIGNING FROM **BRADFORD PARK AVENUE** IN 1946, **LEN SHACKLETON** SCORED SIX GOALS ON HIS DEBUT IN **NEWCASTLE'S** 13-0 DEFEAT OF **NEWPORT COUNTY** -- WITH THREE OF THOSE GOALS COMING WITHIN THE SPACE OF JUST 155 SECONDS!

WHO MADE THESE MEMORABLE DEBUTS?

1 1989: SIGNED FROM **PORTSMOUTH**, HE SCORED FOUR GOALS ON HIS DEBUT IN A 5-2 WIN OVER **LEEDS UNITED** AND WENT ON TO SCORE IN HIS NEXT FIVE LEAGUE GAMES.

2 1998: SIGNED FROM **EVERTON**, HE SCORED TWICE ON HIS DEBUT IN A 3-1 HOME WIN OVER **WIMBLEDON**.

3 2015: A £14.5 MILLION SIGNING FROM **PSV**, HE CAPPED AN IMPRESSIVE DEBUT PERFORMANCE IN MIDFIELD BY SCORING A HEADER FROM A **GABRIEL OBERTAN** CROSS IN A 2-2 DRAW WITH **SOUTHAMPTON**.

4 1982: MIDWAY THROUGH THE SECOND HALF IN HIS DEBUT, THE 31-YEAR-OLD CAPTURE FROM **SOUTHAMPTON** SCORED THE WINNER AGAINST **QPR** AND THE **GALLOWGATE** WENT BANANAS!

5 1995: 83 MINUTES INTO A GAME WHERE **NEWCASTLE** WERE BEATING **COVENTRY CITY** 2-0, THE RECENT SIGNING FROM **QPR** HIT THE FIRST OF HIS 29 GOALS THAT DEBUT SEASON.

6 2019: A STUNNING STRIKE IN THE 72ND MINUTE OF HIS PREMIER LEAGUE DEBUT -- LATER VOTED PREMIER LEAGUE GOAL OF THE MONTH -- GAVE **"THE MAGPIES"** A 1-0 WIN AGAINST **MANCHESTER UNITED**.

7 2012: SENEGALESE SIGNED FROM **FREIBURG**, HE CAME OFF THE BENCH TO SCORE THE WINNER AGAINST **ASTON VILLA**.

8 1971: HIS HOME DEBUT SAW THE RECENT SIGNING FROM *FULHAM* BANG IN A HAT-TRICK AGAINST *LIVERPOOL* BEFORE BEING CARRIED OFF AFTER CLATTERING INTO GOALKEEPER *RAY CLEMENCE* WHILE TRYING TO SCORE HIS FOURTH!

MUNDIAL MAGPIES 1

JUST OVER A YEAR AFTER MAKING HIS *ENGLAND* DEBUT -- IN 1965, AGED ALMOST 30 YEARS OLD -- *JACK CHARLTON* WAS A WORLD CUP-WINNER. HE WENT ON TO REPRESENT HIS COUNTRY IN MEXICO AT THE 1970 WORLD CUP. AS A MANAGER, HE STEERED THE *REPUBLIC OF IRELAND* TO TWO WORLD CUPS, IN 1990 AND 1994.

THESE *NEWCASTLE* PLAYERS OR MANAGERS REPRESENTED THEIR COUNTRY IN A WORLD CUP TOURNAMENT AS A PLAYER. WHICH COUNTRY?

1 *JACKIE MILBURN* (1950)

2 *GEORGE ROBLEDO* (1950)

3 *ROY BENTLEY* (1950)

4 *IVOR BROADIS* (1954)

5 *BILL MCGARRY* (1954)

6 *ALF MCMICHAEL* (1958)

7 *BOBBY ROBSON* (1958)

8 *DICK KEITH* (1958)

9 *IVOR ALLCHURCH* (1958)

10 *TOMMY CASEY* (1958)

11 *KEN LEEK* (1958)

12 *GEORGE EASTHAM* (1962)

13 *STAN ANDERSON* (1962)

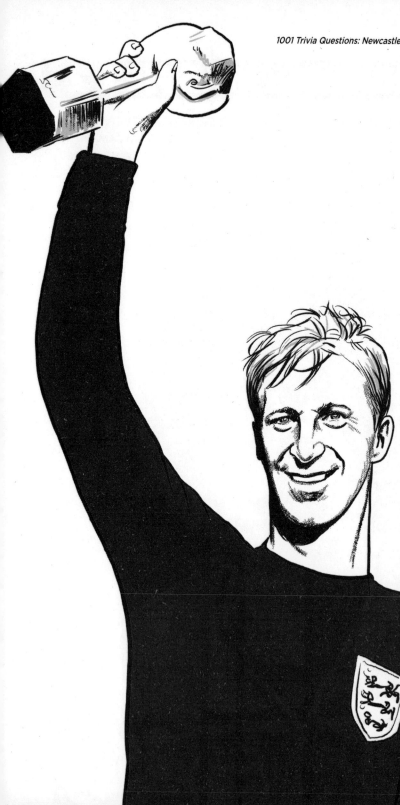

MUNDIAL MAGPIES 2

KEVIN KEEGAN MADE 63 APPEARANCES FOR **ENGLAND** BETWEEN 1972 AND 1982. HIS FINAL APPEARANCE FOR THE NATIONAL TEAM CAME AT THE 1982 WORLD CUP, IN A 0-0 DRAW WITH **SPAIN** THAT **ENGLAND** NEEDED TO WIN IN ORDER TO ADVANCE.

THESE **NEWCASTLE** PLAYERS OR MANAGERS REPRESENTED THEIR COUNTRY IN A WORLD CUP TOURNAMENT AS A PLAYER. WHICH COUNTRY?

1 *JOHN BLACKLEY* (1974)

2 *KENNY DALGLISH* (1974, 1978, 1982)

3 *OSSIE ARDILES* (1978, 1982)

4 *GRAEME SOUNESS* (1978, 1982, 1986)

5 *DAVID MCCREERY* (1982, 1986)

6 *TERRY MCDERMOTT* (1982)

7 *PETER WITHE* (1982)

8 *TOMMY CASSIDY* (1982)

9 *PETER BEARDSLEY* (1986, 1990)

10 *ROY AITKEN* (1986, 1990)

11 *CHRIS WADDLE* (1986, 1990)

12 *JOHN BARNES* (1986, 1990)

13 *IAN STEWART* (1986)

14 *PHILIPPE ALBERT* (1990)

15 *STUART PEARCE* (1990)

16 *DAVID KELLY* (1990)

17 *RUUD GULLIT* (1990)

18 *KEVIN SHEEDY* (1990)

19 *PAUL GASCOIGNE* (1990)

20 *CHRIS HUGHTON* (1990)

MUNDIAL MAGPIES 3

ALAN SHEARER GAINED 63 **ENGLAND** CAPS, CAPTAINING THE TEAM 34 TIMES AND SCORING 30 GOALS, BUT HE ONLY APPEARED IN ONE WORLD CUP TOURNAMENT, LEADING **"THE THREE LIONS"** AT FRANCE 1998.

THESE **NEWCASTLE** PLAYERS OR MANAGERS REPRESENTED THEIR COUNTRY IN A WORLD CUP TOURNAMENT AS A PLAYER. WHICH COUNTRY?

1 **DAVID BATTY** (1998)

2 **DIETMAR HAMANN** (1998, 2002)

3 **RONNY JOHNSEN** (1998)

4 **ROB LEE** (1998)

5 **SILVIO MARIC** (1998)

6 **LES FERDINAND** (1998)

7 **CLARENCE ACUNA** (1998)

8 **MICHAEL OWEN** (1998, 2002)

9 **PATRICK KLUIVERT** (1998)

10 **SOL CAMPBELL** (1998, 2002)

11 **KEVIN GALLACHER** (1998)

12 **STÉPHANE GUIVARC'H** (1998)

13 **CELESTINE BABAYARO** (1998, 2002)

14 **LAMINE DIATTA** (1998)

15 **DARREN JACKSON** (1998)

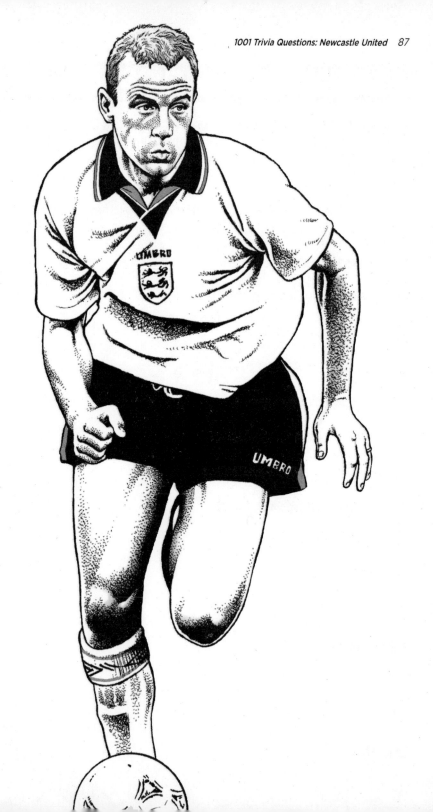

MUNDIAL MAGPIES 4

SHAY GIVEN MADE 134 APPEARANCES OVER A 20-YEAR PERIOD FOR THE **REPUBLIC OF IRELAND** -- BUT THE 2002 TOURNAMENT WAS THE ONLY WORLD CUP IN WHICH **"THE BOYS IN GREEN"** PARTICIPATED DURING THAT TIME.

THESE **NEWCASTLE** PLAYERS OR MANAGERS REPRESENTED THEIR COUNTRY IN A WORLD CUP TOURNAMENT AS A PLAYER. WHICH COUNTRY?

1 **KIERON DYER** (2002)

2 **GEREMI** (2002, 2010)

3 **LAMINE DIATTA** (2002)

4 **ALBERT LUQUE** (2002)

5 **DAMIEN DUFF** (2002)

6 **HUGO VIANA** (2002, 2006)

7 **ANDREAS ANDERSSON** (2002)

8 **EMRE BELÖZOĞLU** (2002)

9 **HABIB BEYE** (2002)

10 **PETER LOVENKRANDS** (2002)

11 **NICKY BUTT** (2002)

12 **ANDY O'BRIEN** (2002)

13 **DIEGO GAVILÁN** (2002, 2006)

14 **JON DAHL TOMASSON** (2002, 2010)

15 **AMDY FAYE** (2002)

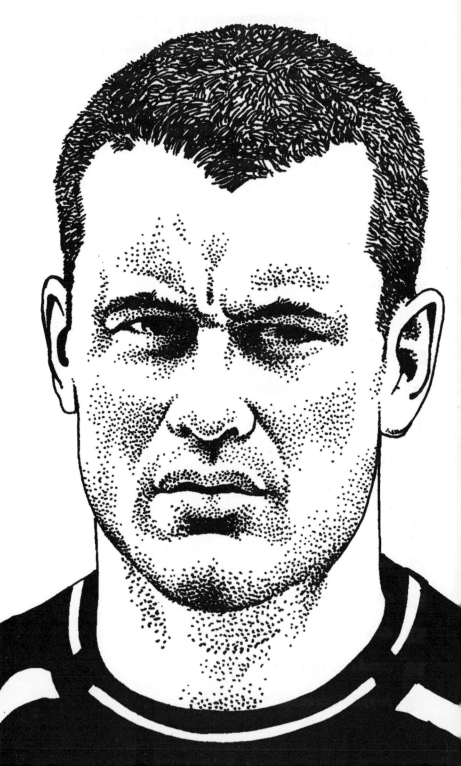

MUNDIAL MAGPIES 5

HAVING WON THE 2001 FIFA WORLD YOUTH CHAMPIONSHIP WITH THE **ARGENTINA** U-20 TEAM AND A GOLD MEDAL AT THE 2004 SUMMER OLYMPICS, **FABRICIO COLOCCINI** REPRESENTED HIS COUNTRY AT THE 2004 COPA AMÉRICA AND THE 2006 WORLD CUP.

THESE **NEWCASTLE** PLAYERS OR MANAGERS REPRESENTED THEIR COUNTRY IN A WORLD CUP TOURNAMENT AS A PLAYER. WHICH COUNTRY?

1 **OGUCHI ONYEWU** (2006, 2010)

2 **JERMAINE JENAS** (2006)

3 **SHAKA HISLOP** (2006)

4 **MARK VIDUKA** (2006)

5 **MICHAEL CARRICK** (2006, 2010)

6 **JEAN-ALAIN BOUMSONG** (2006)

7 **DAVID ROZEHNAL** (2006)

8 **LOUIS SAHA** (2006)

9 **CRAIG MOORE** (2006, 2010)

10 **CHEICK TIOTÉ** (2010, 2014)

11 **NACHO GONZÁLEZ** (2010)

12 **OBAFEMI MARTINS** (2010)

13 **SÉBASTIEN BASSONG** (2010)

14 **JONÁS GUTIÉRREZ** (2010)

15 **SEYDOU DOUMBIA** (2010)

16 *JAMES MILNER*
(2010, 2014)

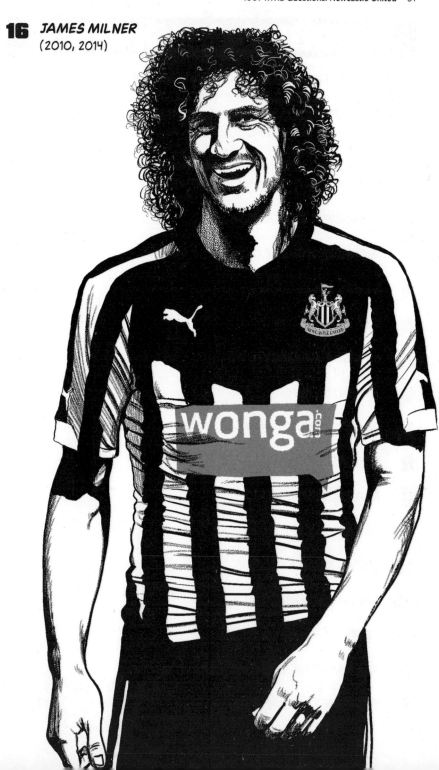

MUNDIAL MAGPIES 6

2013 ALGERIAN FOOTBALLER OF THE YEAR, *ISLAM SLIMANI* PLAYED FOR **ALGERIA** AT WORLD CUP 2014 AND WAS PART OF THE TEAM THAT WON THE 2019 AFRICA CUP OF NATIONS. DURING WORLD CUP 2022 QUALIFICATION HE BECAME HIS COUNTRY'S ALL-TIME TOP GOALSCORER.

THESE **NEWCASTLE** PLAYERS OR MANAGERS REPRESENTED THEIR COUNTRY IN A WORLD CUP TOURNAMENT AS A PLAYER. WHICH COUNTRY?

1 *GEORGINIO WIJNALDUM* (2014)

2 *MATHIEU DEBUCHY* (2014)

3 *JAMES TROISI* (2014)

4 *DEANDRE YEDLIN* (2014)

5 *MOUSSA SISSOKO* (2014)

6 *TIM KRUL* (2014)

7 *CHRISTIAN ATSU* (2014)

8 *LOIC REMY* (2014)

9 *FRASER FORSTER* (2014)

10 *YOHAN CABAYE* (2014)

11 *DARYL JANMAAT* (2014)

12 *SHOLA AMEOBI* (2014)

13 *RÉMY CABELLA* (2014)

14 *ALEKSANDAR MITROVIĆ* (2018)

15 *FLORIAN THAUVIN* (2018)

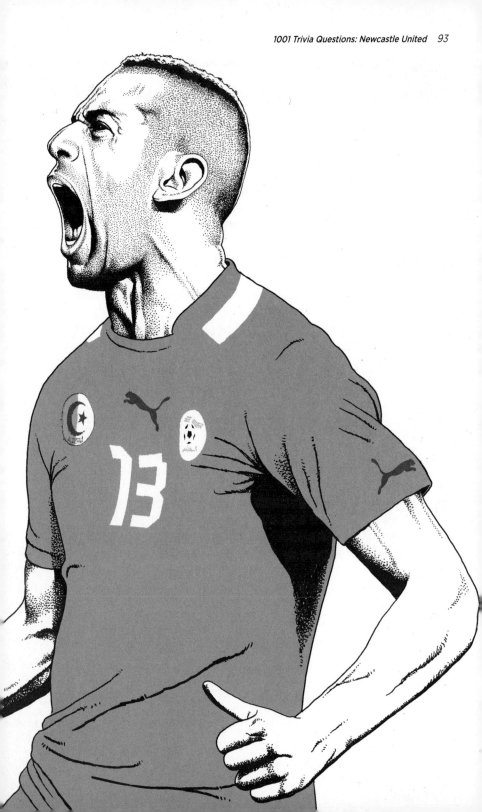

THE YOUNG ONES

IN ADDITION TO GAINING 61 FULL *ENGLAND* CAPS, BETWEEN 2004 AND 2009 *JAMES MILNER* MADE A RECORD 46 APPEARANCES FOR THE *ENGLAND U-21* TEAM.

1   WHICH £7 MILLION *NEWCASTLE* SIGNING FROM *WIMBLEDON* IN 2000 MADE 14 APPEARANCES FOR THE *ENGLAND U-21* SIDE BUT NEVER GAINED A FULL *ENGLAND* CAP?

2   WHICH FORMER *NEWCASTLE* PLAYER COACHED THE ENGLAND U-21 TEAM THAT FINISHED RUNNERS-UP IN THE 2009 UEFA EUROPEAN UNDER-21 CHAMPIONSHIP, LOSING TO *GERMANY* IN THE FINAL?

3   WHICH DEFENDER, WHOSE CLUBS INCLUDE *NEWCASTLE, PARIS SAINT-GERMAIN, LILLE, LAZIO* AND *HAMBURGER SV*, WAS A MEMBER OF THE *CZECH REPUBLIC* TEAM THAT WON THE 2002 UEFA EUROPEAN UNDER-21 CHAMPIONSHIP?

4   WHICH NIGERIAN-BORN FORWARD HIT 7 GOALS IN 20 GAMES AT U-21 LEVEL FOR *ENGLAND* BUT WAS NEVER CALLED UP FOR THE SENIOR TEAM AND EVENTUALLY SWITCHED HIS ALLEGIANCE TO *NIGERIA* AT THE AGE OF 30 IN 2011?

5   WHICH *NEWCASTLE* PLAYER RACKED UP 13 GOALS FOR *ENGLAND* (SCORED IN JUST 11 APPEARANCES) AT U-21 LEVEL, A RECORD THAT WAS SUBSEQUENTLY MATCHED BY *FRANCIS JEFFERS* AND EVENTUALLY BROKEN BY *EDDIE NKETIAH*?

6   WHICH *NEWCASTLE* STRIKER, DURING HIS *WEST HAM* DAYS, SCORED ONE OF THE GOALS THAT HELPED *ENGLAND* BEAT *WEST GERMANY* 5-4 ON AGGREGATE TO WIN THE 1982 UEFA EUROPEAN UNDER-21 CHAMPIONSHIP?

7   WHICH *NEWCASTLE* DEFENDER PLAYED 268 TIMES FOR THE CLUB OVER 13 SEASONS BETWEEN 2003 AND 2016, AND CAPTAINED THE *ENGLAND U-21* SIDE -- FOR WHOM HE MADE 29 APPEARANCES -- BUT DESPITE CALL-UPS TO THE SENIOR SQUAD, NEVER EARNED A FULL *ENGLAND* CAP?

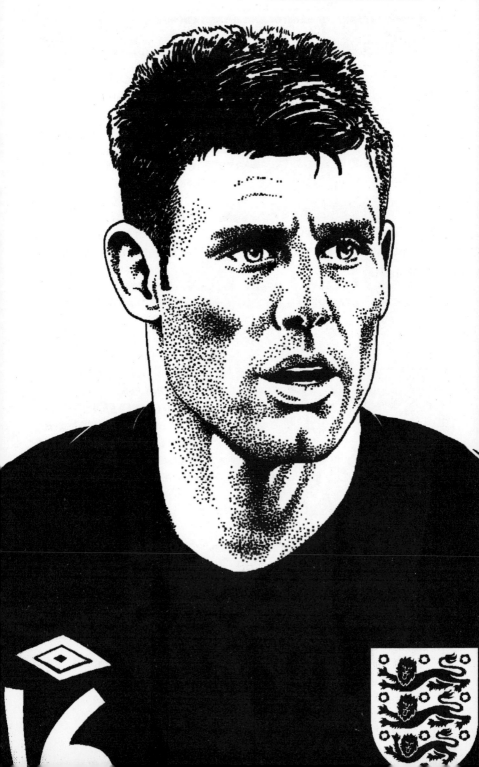

HOT SEATS

BORN IN AMSTERDAM IN 1962, **RUUD GULLIT** MADE HIS DEBUT FOR **NETHERLANDS** AT THE AGE OF 19, WHILE PLAYING FOR **HAARLEM**. AFTER SPELLS AT **FEYENOORD** AND **PSV EINDHOVEN**, HE JOINED **AC MILAN** IN 1987, THE YEAR HE WAS VOTED BOTH WORLD AND EUROPEAN FOOTBALLER OF THE YEAR. IN 1988, HE WON A SERIE A TITLE WITH **MILAN** AND CAPTAINED HIS COUNTRY TO VICTORY IN THE UEFA EUROPEAN CHAMPIONSHIP. HAVING SPENT TWO SPELLS AT **SAMPDORIA**, HE MOVED TO **CHELSEA**, WHERE HE SOON SUCCEEDED **GLENN HODDLE** TO BECOME PLAYER/MANAGER. WITH **CHELSEA'S** 1997 FA CUP FINAL VICTORY OVER **MIDDLESBROUGH, GULLIT** BECAME THE FIRST FOREIGN MANAGER TO LIFT THE TROPHY.

WHO DID THE FOLLOWING SUCCEED AS MANAGER?

1 *OSSIE ARDILES -- WEST BROMWICH ALBION,* 1992

2 *KENNY DALGLISH -- BLACKBURN ROVERS,* 1991

3 *SAM ALLARDYCE -- SUNDERLAND,* 2015

4 *ALAN PARDEW -- WEST BROMWICH ALBION,* 2017

5 *ARTHUR COX -- DERBY COUNTY,* 1984

6 *KEVIN KEEGAN -- MANCHESTER CITY,* 2001

7 *RAFAEL BENÍTEZ -- REAL MADRID,* 2015

8 *STEVE MCCLAREN -- QUEENS PARK RANGERS,* 2018

9 *STEVE BRUCE -- ASTON VILLA,* 2016

10 *GLENN ROEDER -- WEST HAM UNITED,* 2001

SOUNESS SPENDINGS

20,000 FANS THRONGED **ST JAMES' PARK** FOR THE OFFICIAL UNVEILING OF **MICHAEL OWEN** AS A **NEWCASTLE** PLAYER IN 2005. THE BALLON D'OR WINNER'S £16.8 MILLION SIGNING FROM **REAL MADRID** MADE HIM THE CLUB'S RECORD ACQUISITION TO THAT POINT.

OWEN WAS A **GRAEME SOUNESS** SIGNING -- AS WERE:

1   AUGUST, 2005: £9 MILLION FROM *DEPORTIVO DE LA CORUÑA*

2   DECEMBER, 2004: £8 MILLION FROM *RANGERS*

3   JULY, 2005: £6 MILLION FROM *CHELSEA*

4   JULY, 2005: £3.8 MILLION FROM *INTER MILAN*

5   JANUARY, 2005: £2 MILLION FROM *PORTSMOUTH*

6   AUGUST, 2005: £1.5 MILLION FROM *ASTON VILLA*

7   JANUARY, 2005: UNDISCLOSED FEE FROM *CHELSEA*

8   JULY, 2005: FREE TRANSFER FROM *BORUSSIA MÖNCHENGLADBACH*

9   JULY, 2005: FREE TRANSFER FROM *FULHAM*

AUSSIE MAGPIES

HAVING WON FOUR EREDIVISIE TITLES AND THE KNVB CUP WITH *AJAX*, *SIEM DE JONG* JOINED *NEWCASTLE* IN 2014. HIS THREE SEASONS ON TYNESIDE WERE DOGGED BY INJURIES, RANGING FROM A COLLAPSED LUNG TO A FREAK ACCIDENT IN WHICH ONE OF HIS CONTACT LENSES WAS PUSHED INTO HIS EYE. AFTER RETURNING TO *AJAX* HE SPENT TIME ON LOAN IN AUSTRALIA WITH *SYDNEY FC*, DURING WHICH HE PLAYED IN THE TEAM THAT WON THE 2019 A-LEAGUE GRAND FINAL.

WITH WHICH AUSTRALIAN TEAM DID THE FOLLOWING PLAY:

1 *DAMIEN DUFF*

2 *PETER BEARDSLEY*

3 *GRAEME SOUNESS*

4 *MARK VIDUKA*

5 *AARON HUGHES*

6 *KEVIN KEEGAN*

7 *RON MCGARRY*

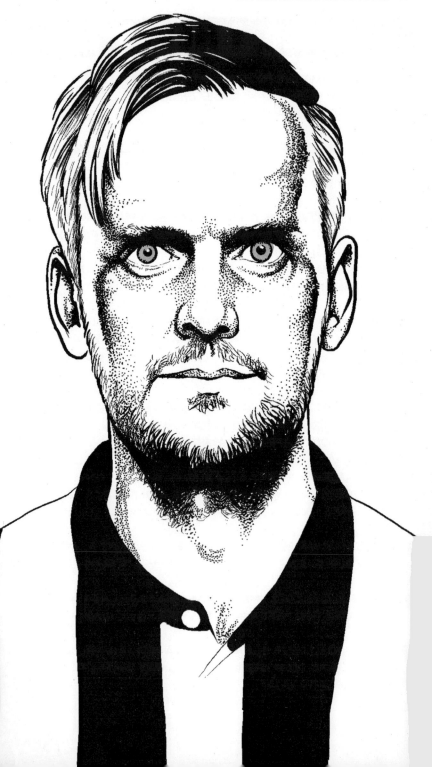

WELL, I NEVER ...

WHILE PLAYING AMATEUR FOOTBALL WITH **TOW LAW** AND TRYING TO BREAK INTO THE PROFESSIONAL GAME, **CHRIS WADDLE** WORKED IN A SAUSAGE SEASONING FACTORY.

1 WHICH **NEWCASTLE, QPR, CHELSEA** AND **BOURNEMOUTH** MIDFIELDER STUDIED THEOLOGY AND BECAME A PASTOR AT THE CALVARY GRACE CHURCH IN CALGARY, CANADA?

2 WHICH **NEWCASTLE, CARDIFF CITY, SUNDERLAND** AND **IPSWICH TOWN** STRIKER'S ACTUAL FIRST NAME IS **ROCKY?**

3 WHICH **NEWCASTLE** AND **BELGIUM** STAR BECAME A FRUIT AND VEG SELLER WHEN HIS PLAYING DAYS WERE OVER?

4 INSPIRED BY A 1960S TV WESTERN CALLED **"HAVE GUN -- WILL TRAVEL"** STARRING **RICHARD BOONE**, WHICH **NEWCASTLE** STRIKER CARRIED CARDS WITH THE MOTTO **"HAVE GOALS WILL TRAVEL"** PRINTED ON THEM?

5 WHO TEAMED UP WITH REGGAE BAND **REVELATION TIME** AND HIT THE TOP THREE ON THE DUTCH TOP 40 WITH THE ANTI-APARTHEID SONG **"SOUTH AFRICA"** IN 1988?

6 WHICH FORMER **NEWCASTLE** STRIKER, A TREBLE WINNER WITH **RANGERS** AND A WORLD CUP WINNER WITH **FRANCE**, BECAME A SWIMMING POOL SALESMAN IN HIS HOMETOWN OF CONCARNEAU?

7 WHICH FORMER **NEWCASTLE** MIDFIELDER BOUGHT A CARP FISHING LAKE BUSINESS IN FRANCE WHICH HE RENAMED **"ETANG DE BOWS"**?

8 WHICH PLAYER ONCE LAUNCHED A BUSINESS SELLING FLAVOURED CONDOMS THAT WERE MARKETED UNDER HIS NICKNAME?

9 WHICH GOALKEEPER GRADUATED WITH A DEGREE IN MECHANICAL ENGINEERING FROM WASHINGTON'S HOWARD UNIVERSITY AND INTERNED WITH NASA?

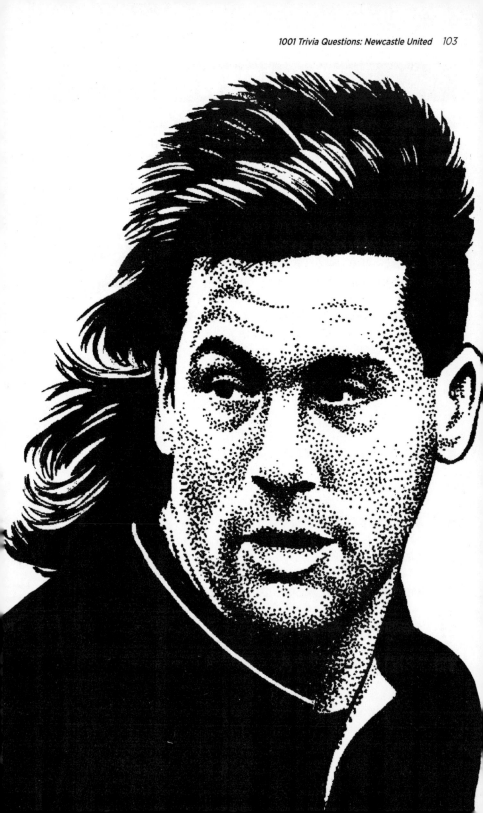

NUMBER 9

ALAN SHEARER FAMOUSLY WORE THE NUMBER 9 SHIRT FOR **NEWCASTLE** AND **ENGLAND** ... BUT WHEN HE MADE HIS **ENGLAND** DEBUT, AGAINST **FRANCE** IN FEBRUARY, OF 1992, HE ACTUALLY WORE THE NUMBER 10 SHIRT. **ENGLAND** WON 2-0 ... AND **SHEARER** SCORED.

CAN YOU NAME THE OTHER PLAYERS IN THAT **ENGLAND** TEAM FROM THEIR SHIRT NUMBER AND THE CLUB THEY PLAYED FOR AT THE TIME?

1 **SHEFFIELD WEDNESDAY**

2 **LIVERPOOL**

3 **NOTTINGHAM FOREST** (CAPTAIN)

4 **EVERTON**

5 **NOTTINGHAM FOREST**

6 **LIVERPOOL**

7 **MANCHESTER UNITED**

8 **CRYSTAL PALACE**

9 **NOTTINGHAM FOREST**

11 **SHEFFIELD WEDNESDAY**

12 **TOTTENHAM HOTSPUR** (SCORED THE OTHER GOAL)

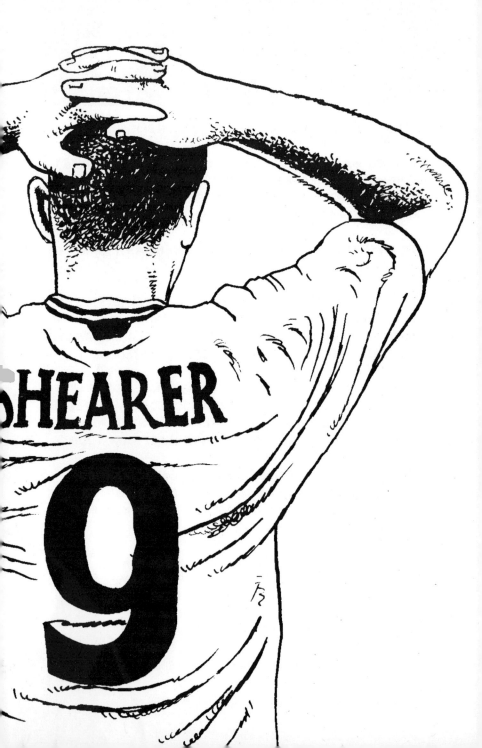

"YOU'LL NOT SEE NOTHING LIKE THE MIGHTY WYN ..."

ONE OF THE MOST POWERFUL HEADERS OF A BALL IN BRITISH FOOTBALL HISTORY, **WYN DAVIES** ESTABLISHED HIS TARGET-MAN CREDENTIALS WITH **BOLTON WANDERERS**, BEFORE SIGNING FOR **"THE MAGPIES"** IN 1966. HAVING WON THE FAIRS CUP WITH **NEWCASTLE**, THE **WALES** INTERNATIONAL PLAYED FOR BOTH MANCHESTER CLUBS AND **BLACKPOOL** BEFORE HIS CAREER GRADUALLY WOUND DOWN IN THE LOWER LEAGUES.

IDENTIFY THESE OTHERS WHO PLAYED FOR BOTH **NEWCASTLE** AND **BOLTON WANDERERS**:

1 LEFT-BACK WHOSE TWO LENGTHY SPELLS WITH **NEWCASTLE** CAME EITHER SIDE OF HIS FOUR YEARS WITH **BOLTON**, FOR WHOM HE WAS A CLUB RECORD £2.5 MILLION SIGNING IN 1997. HE LATER PLAYED FOR **SUNDERLAND**, **LEEDS** AND **HARTLEPOOL UNITED**.

2 HAVING PROMOTION TO THE PREMIER LEAGUE IN HIS DECADE WITH **BOLTON**, THE LIVERPUDLIAN MIDFIELDER JOINED **NEWCASTLE** IN 2009. RELEGATION WAS FOLLOWED BY AN IMMEDIATE RETURN TO THE TOP FLIGHT, BEFORE HE MOVED ON TO **WEST HAM** IN 2011.

3 SENEGALESE DEFENDER WHO JOINED **BOLTON** FROM **LENS** IN 2005, MOVING ON TO **NEWCASTLE** IN 2007. HE SIGNED FOR **STOKE CITY** THE FOLLOWING SEASON, LATER JOINING **WEST HAM UNITED** AND **HULL CITY**.

4 GEORDIE LAD WHO LEFT **NEWCASTLE** FOR **BOLTON** IN 1993, WHERE HE WAS AN INTEGRAL PART OF THE TEAMS THAT WON TWO PROMOTIONS AND REACHED THE LEAGUE CUP FINAL. A SPELL AT **ASTON VILLA** WAS FOLLOWED BY A MOVE TO **CELTIC**, WITH WHOM HE WON MULTIPLE HONOURS, INCLUDING FOUR LEAGUE TITLES AND FOUR DOMESTIC CUPS, AND REACHED THE UEFA CUP FINAL IN 2003. HE PLAYED FOR **LEEDS** AND **HARTLEPOOL** BEFORE RETIRING.

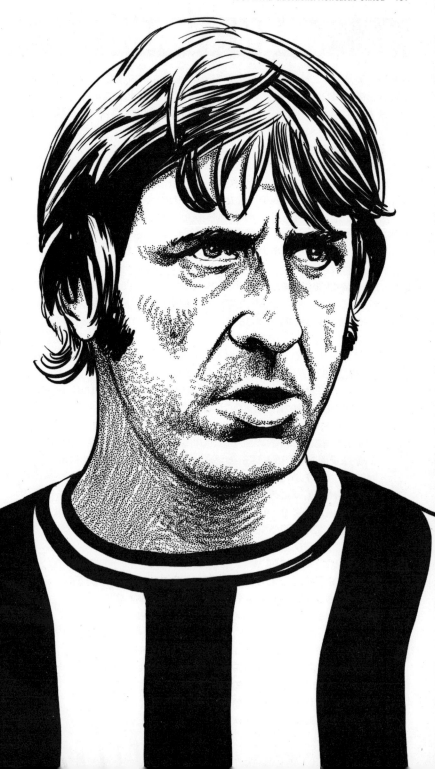

TEEN TITANS

ANDY CARROLL MADE HIS FIRST-TEAM DEBUT FOR **NEWCASTLE** ON NOVEMBER 2, 2006, AT THE AGE OF 17 YEARS AND 300 DAYS, COMING ON AS A LATE SUBSTITUTE FOR **NOLBERTO SOLANO** IN A 1-0 UEFA CUP WIN OVER **PALERMO**. THE APPEARANCE MADE HIM THE YOUNGEST-EVER PLAYER TO REPRESENT **"THE MAGPIES"** IN EUROPE TO THAT POINT. THE YOUNGEST PLAYER TO REPRESENT **NEWCASTLE** IS **STEVE WATSON**, WHO WAS ONLY 16 YEARS AND 233 DAYS OLD WHEN HE MADE HIS DEBUT IN A LEAGUE GAME AGAINST **WOLVES** IN 1990.

IDENTIFY THE FOLLOWING WHO WERE ALL 17 YEARS OLD WHEN THEY PLAYED THEIR FIRST GAME FOR **NEWCASTLE:**

1 **SLOVENIA** INTERNATIONAL, DEBUTED IN 2009 AND WENT ON TO PLAY ON LOAN AT **CARDIFF, ROTHERHAM, RANGERS, WIGAN** AND **BRADFORD CITY** BEFORE JOINING DUTCH SIDE **TWENTE** IN 2017.

2 LEFT-BACK WHO DEBUTED IN 1991, HE HAD TWO SPELLS AT **NEWCASTLE** -- EITHER SIDE OF FOUR SEASONS WITH **BOLTON WANDERERS** -- BEFORE PLAYING FOR **SUNDERLAND, LEEDS UNITED** AND **HARTLEPOOL UNITED.**

3 HAVING DEBUTED AS A SUBSTITUTE AGAINST **MANCHESTER UNITED** IN 1989, CENTRE-BACK WHO WON A FIRST DIVISION TITLE IN 1993 AND PLAYED IN THE 1998 FA CUP FINAL, BEFORE JOINING **MANCHESTER CITY** IN A £2 MILLION DEAL IN 2000. RELEGATION WAS FOLLOWED BY AN IMMEDIATE RETURN TO THE PREMIER LEAGUE, AFTER WHICH HE JOINED **LEICESTER CITY.**

4 ZAIRE-BORN WINGER WHO DEBUTED IN 1998, HE WENT ON TO PLAY FOR **BRIGHTON & HOVE ALBION, DONCASTER ROVERS, QPR, SUNDERLAND** AND **LUTON TOWN,** BEFORE HEADING TO TURKEY.

5 CAPTAIN OF THE SIDE THAT WON THE 1985 FA YOUTH CUP, HE MADE HIS FIRST-TEAM DEBUT AS A SUB IN A 1-0 WIN OVER **QPR** ON APRIL 13, 1985. THREE YEARS LATER, HE LEFT IN A £2.2 MILLION TRANSFER.

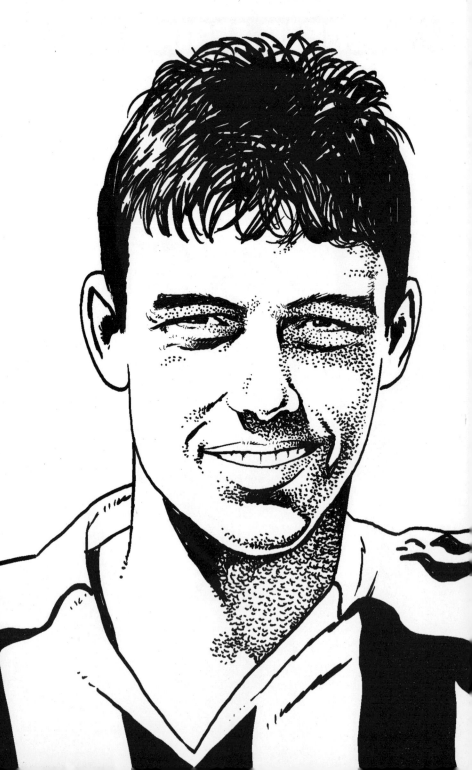

WORLD LEADERS

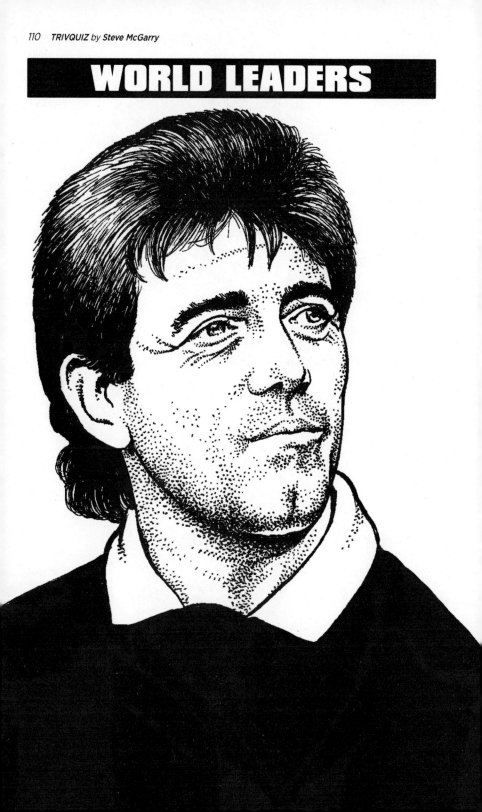

KEVIN KEEGAN SUCCEEDED **GLENN HODDLE** AS **ENGLAND** MANAGER IN FEBRUARY, 1999. HE MANAGED TO STEER THE TEAM TO EURO 2000 BUT THE TOURNAMENT PERFORMANCES WERE UNDERWHELMING ... AND WHEN, IN OCTOBER OF 2020, **ENGLAND** LOST THE FIRST GAME IN THE WORLD CUP QUALIFIERS, **KEEGAN** RESIGNED. **NEWCASTLE'S** CONNECTION TO THE **ENGLAND** MANAGER JOB IS STRONG. THREE OTHER **NEWCASTLE** MANAGERS -- **BOBBY ROBSON, STEVE MCCLAREN** AND **SAM ALLARDYCE** -- HAVE HELD THE POSITION, AND FORMER **NEWCASTLE** PLAYER **STUART PEARCE** SERVED BRIEFLY AS CARETAKER BOSS.

WHICH **NEWCASTLE** PLAYERS OR MANAGERS SERVED AS BOSS OF THE FOLLOWING NATIONAL TEAMS?

1   **MONTSERRAT** (2004)

2   **SAUDI ARABIA** (1976-1977)

3   **THAILAND** (1998-2003)

4   **JAMAICA** (2008-2009)

5   **GUAM** (1998-2003)

6   **NORTHERN IRELAND** (2011-2020)

7   **CURAÇAO** (2015-2016)

8   **ZAMBIA** (1982-1983)

9   **INDIA** (1984)

10   **GEORGIA** (2009-2014)

11   **NEPAL** (1987)

12   **INDONESIA** (2004-2007)

MAGPIES & CANARIES

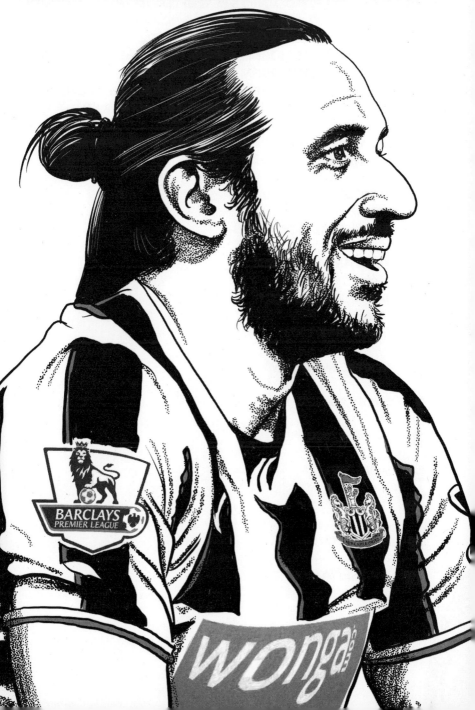

JONÁS GUTIÉRREZ JOINED *NEWCASTLE* FROM *MALLORCA* IN 2008, WINNING THE CHAMPIONSHIP TITLE IN 2010. HIS SEVEN SEASONS ON TYNESIDE WERE DISRUPTED BY TESTICULAR CANCER, FROM WHICH HE MADE A FULL RECOVERY. HE SCORED 12 GOALS IN 205 MATCHES ACROSS ALL COMPETITIONS FOR *"THE MAGPIES"* -- INCLUDING THE GOAL IN 2015 WHICH KEPT THEM IN THE PREMIER LEAGUE -- BEFORE JOINING *DEPORTIVO DE LA CORUÑA.*

GUTIÉRREZ SPENT TIME ON LOAN AT *NORWICH CITY* IN 2014. IDENTIFY THESE OTHERS WHO ALSO PLAYED FOR *"THE CANARIES"*:

1 CAMEROON DEFENDER, BORN IN FRANCE, WHO JOINED *NEWCASTLE* FROM *METZ* IN 2008, MOVING ON TO *SPURS* THE FOLLOWING SEASON IN AN £8 MILLION DEAL. HE SIGNED FOR *NORWICH* IN 2012 AND IN FIVE SEASONS WITH THE CLUB, WAS RELEGATED AND PROMOTED.

2 *ENGLAND* GOALKEEPER WHO SPENT THE FIRST FEW YEARS OF HIS CAREER WITH *NEWCASTLE*, DURING WHICH TIME HE WON THE 2010 LEAGUE ONE TITLE WHILE ON LOAN AT *NORWICH*. HE WON FOUR LEAGUE TITLES AND THREE DOMESTIC CUPS WITH *CELTIC* BEFORE JOINING *SOUTHAMPTON* IN 2014.

3 HAVING PLAYED UNDER HIS MANAGER FATHER AT *NEWCASTLE*, HE JOINED *NORWICH* IN 2009. HIS SUBSEQUENT COACHING AND MANAGEMENT CAREER HAS SEEN HIM WIN HONOURS WITH A NUMBER OF TEAMS IN U.S. SOCCER, INCLUDING *MIAMI FC.*

4 MIDFIELDER WHO JOINED *NEWCASTLE* IN 1978 AFTER A CAREER THAT HAD SEEN HIM PLAY MORE THAN 400 GAMES WITH *SUNDERLAND, WEST BROMWICH ALBION* AND *NORWICH.*

5 *SCOTLAND* INTERNATIONAL WHO SPENT SEVEN SEASONS WITH *BLACKBURN ROVERS* BEFORE JOINING *NEWCASTLE* IN 2016. HE WON A CHAMPIONSHIP TITLE IN HIS ONE SEASON WITH *"THE MAGPIES"*, BEFORE JOINING *NORWICH*, WHERE HE HAS YO-YOED BETWEEN THE CHAMPIONSHIP AND PREMIER LEAGUE.

6 WINGER WHO CAME THROUGH THE RANKS AT *NORWICH* WITH HIS TWIN BROTHER, *JOSH.* HE JOINED *NEWCASTLE* IN 2017, A YEAR BEFORE HIS BROTHER LEFT FOR *NORWICH* FOR *CARDIFF CITY.*

"CATCH ME IF YOU CAN, 'CAUSE I'M THE ENGLAND MAN ..."

SON OF AN ARMY COLONEL WHO CAPTAINED THE *JAMAICA* NATIONAL FOOTBALL TEAM AND FORMED JAMAICA'S FIRST BOBSLEIGH TEAM, *JOHN BARNES* WAS BORN IN JAMAICA. HE MOVED TO ENGLAND AT THE AGE OF 12, AFTER HIS FATHER WAS APPOINTED DEFENCE ADVISER TO THE HIGH COMMISSION OF JAMAICA. *JOHN* WENT ON TO WIN 79 *ENGLAND* CAPS.

WHICH COUNTRY HAVE THE FOLLOWING PLAYERS REPRESENTED AT FULL INTERNATIONAL LEVEL?

1 *CARL CORT*

2 *VURNON ANITA*

3 *GAËL BIGIRIMANA*

4 *LOMANA LUALUA*

5 *EMMANUEL RIVIÈRE*

6 *GEORGE ROBLEDO*

7 *MATZ SELS*

8 *SHEFKI KUQI*

9 *MASSADIO HAÏDARA*

10 *NIKODIMOS PAPAVASILIOU*

11 *RUEL FOX*

12 *OGUCHI ONYEWU*

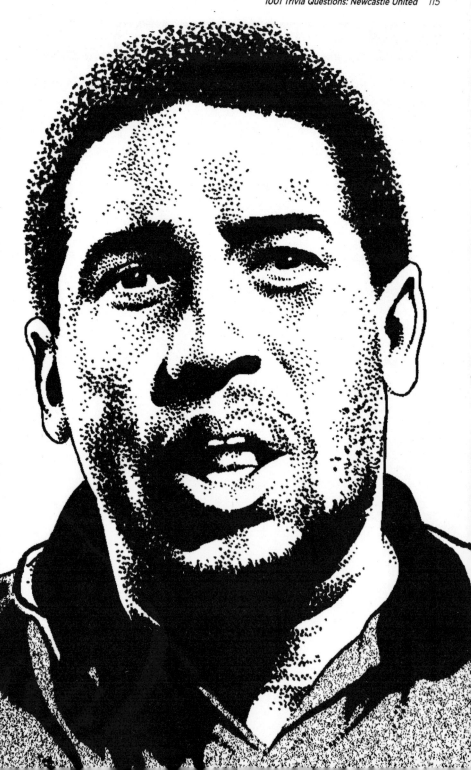

COUNTRY LIFE

KENNY SANSOM MADE 86 APPEARANCES FOR **ENGLAND**, INCLUDING 59 GAMES UNDER SUBSEQUENT **NEWCASTLE** BOSS **BOBBY ROBSON**.

UNDER WHICH PAST OR FUTURE **NEWCASTLE** MANAGER DID THE FOLLOWING MAKE AN INTERNATIONAL APPEARANCE IN THE YEAR SHOWN?

1 **DANNY ROSE -- ENGLAND**, 2016

2 **ANDREW COLE -- ENGLAND**, 1999

3 **JOHN ANDERSON -- REPUBLIC OF IRELAND**, 1986

4 **JOHN BARNES -- ENGLAND**, 1983

5 **ALAN SMITH -- ENGLAND**, 2007

6 **RYAN FRASER -- SCOTLAND**, 2020

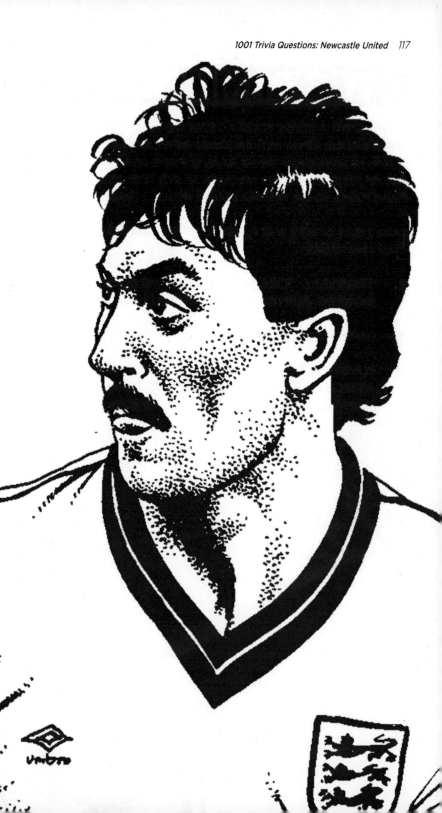

IT'S HAMMER TIME!

HAVING SPENT A DOZEN YEARS -- FROM THE AGE OF 16 -- AT *BOLTON WANDERERS, KEVIN NOLAN* JOINED *NEWCASTLE* IN EARLY 2009. IN 2011, HE SIGNED FOR *WEST HAM*, TEAMING UP AGAIN WITH *SAM ALLARDYCE*, HIS FORMER MANAGER AT *BOLTON. NOLAN* WON PROMOTIONS TO THE PREMIER LEAGUE WITH ALL THREE TEAMS.

NAME THESE OTHERS WHO PLAYED FOR *"THE MAGPIES"* AND *"THE HAMMERS"*:

1   *TRINIDAD & TOBAGO* GOALKEEPER, HIS OTHER CLUBS INCLUDE *READING, PORTSMOUTH* AND *FC DALLAS*.

2   CAPPED 95 TIMES BY *PERU*.

3   PLAYED FOR *CHARLTON ATHLETIC, LEEDS, WEST HAM, NEWCASTLE, BIRMINGHAM CITY* AND *IPSWICH TOWN*, MANAGED *CHARLTON* BEFORE TAKING THE REINS AT *BIRMINGHAM*.

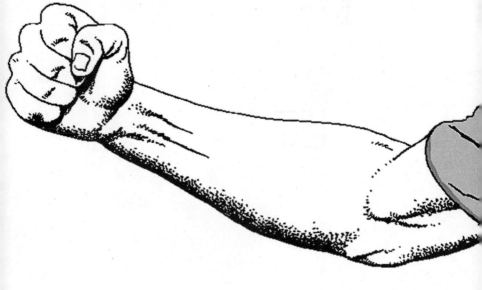

4   PROLIFIC CENTRE-FORWARD WHO MADE HIS NAME AT *COLCHESTER UNITED*, HE WON THE 1955 FA CUP WITH *NEWCASTLE* AND THE SECOND DIVISION TITLE WITH *WEST HAM*.

5 FRENCH-BORN *SENEGAL* STRIKER WHOSE OTHER CLUBS INCLUDE *CHELSEA, BEŞIKTAŞ* AND *SHANGHAI SHENHUA*.

6 CAPPED 33 TIMES BY *ENGLAND*, HIS OTHER CLUBS INCLUDED *IPSWICH TOWN, QUEENS PARK RANGERS* AND *MIDDLESBROUGH*. IN 2021, A COLLAPSED LUNG SAW HIM WITHDRAWN DURING THE THIRD SERIES OF *"CELEBRITY SAS: WHO DARES WINS"*.

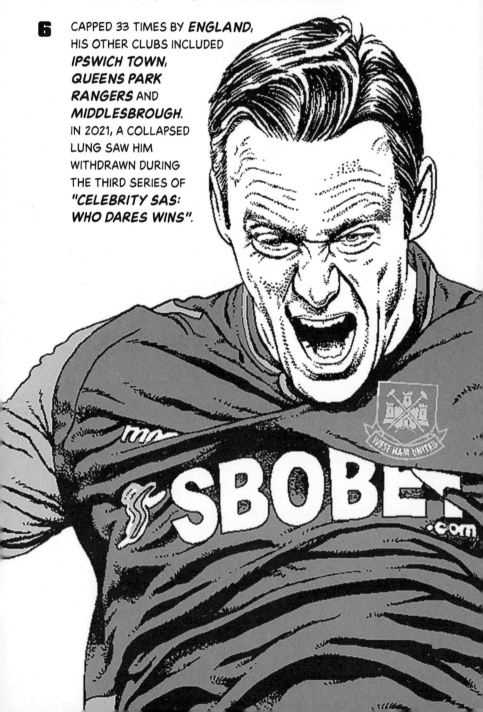

THE GOAL MERCHANTS

MALCOLM MACDONALD ARRIVED ON TYNESIDE IN 1971 AND SCORED 30 GOALS TO ESTABLISH HIMSELF AS **NEWCASTLE'S** TOP SCORER IN HIS DEBUT SEASON. HE TOPPED THE CLUB'S GOALSCORING CHARTS FOR THE NEXT THREE SEASONS ... HITTING 32 GOALS IN 1974-75, INCLUDING 25 IN THE LEAGUE, WHICH EARNED HIM THE GOLDEN BOOT. **ALAN SHEARER** WAS TOP **NEWCASTLE** GOALSCORER IN TEN CONSECUTIVE SEASONS.

IDENTIFY THESE OTHERS WHO SUBSEQUENTLY TOPPED **NEWCASTLE'S** GOALSCORING CHARTS ON MULTIPLE OCCASIONS:

1 1976-77: 17 GOALS AND 1977-78: 16 GOALS -- **BLACKPOOL** GREAT, PLAYED IN THE 1976 LEAGUE CUP FINAL FOR **NEWCASTLE**

2 1981-82: 20 GOALS AND 1982-83: 22 GOALS -- SIGNED FROM **EVERTON**, HE LATER PLAYED FOR **SHEFFIELD WEDNESDAY**, **WEST BROM**, **MANCHESTER CITY** AND **LEEDS UNITED**

3 1984-85: 13 GOALS AND 1985-86: 10 GOALS -- PLAYED FOR **LIVERPOOL** AND **EVERTON** IN BETWEEN TWO SPELLS AT **NEWCASTLE** BEFORE PLAYING FOR **BOLTON** AND MORE

4 1984-85: 13 GOALS AND 1985-86: 10 GOALS -- THE FIRST BRAZILIAN TO PLAY IN ENGLISH FOOTBALL

5 1989-90: 36 GOALS AND 1990-91: 20 GOALS -- SIGNED FROM **PORTSMOUTH**, HE LATER MOVED ON TO **COVENTRY CITY**

6 1993-94: 41 GOALS AND 1994-95: 15 GOALS -- **ENGLAND** STRIKER WHO SUBSEQUENTLY WON THE CHAMPIONS LEAGUE

7 2007-08: 13 GOALS AND 2008-09: 10 GOALS -- **ENGLAND** STRIKER FORMERLY OF **LIVERPOOL** AND **REAL MADRID**

8 2011-12: 16 GOALS AND 2012-13: 13 GOALS -- **SENEGAL** STRIKER, SIGNED FROM **WEST HAM**, LATER MOVED TO **CHELSEA**

9 2017-18: 10 GOALS AND 2018-19: 13 GOALS -- MOVED ON TO **LEICESTER CITY** IN 2019

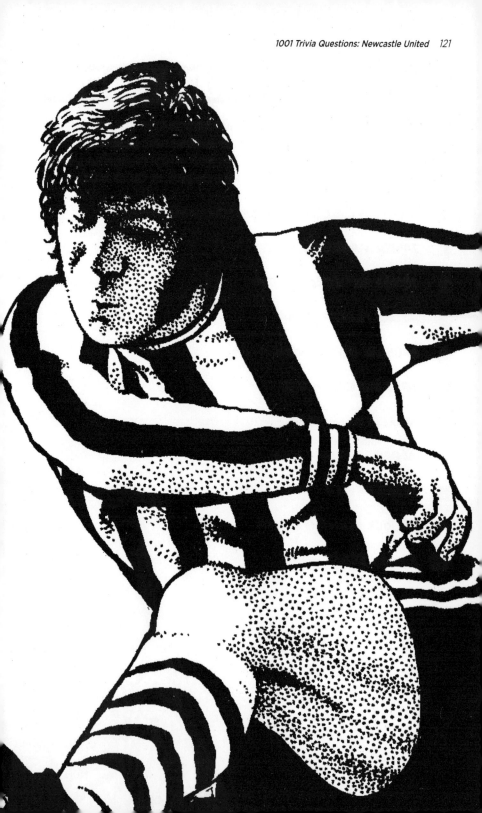

IMPORTED FROM SPAIN

KIERAN TRIPPIER, THE BURY-BORN RIGHT-BACK WHOSE CAREER HAS TAKEN HIM FROM **MANCHESTER CITY** TO **BARNSLEY, BURNLEY, SPURS** AND THEN **ATLÉTICO MADRID** -- WITH WHOM HE WON LA LIGA IN 2021 -- JOINED **NEWCASTLE** IN A £12 MILLION DEAL IN EARLY 2022.

FROM WHICH SPANISH CLUBS WERE THE FOLLOWING SIGNED:

1 *JAVIER MANQUILLO* -- 2017

2 *JONÁS GUTIÉRREZ* -- 2008

3 *AYOZE PÉREZ* -- 2014

4 *MICHAEL OWEN* -- 2005

5 *JOSÉ ENRIQUE* -- 2007

6 *MARCELINO* -- 1999

7 *ALBERT LUQUE* -- 2005

8 *JESÚS GÁMEZ* -- 2016

9 *PATRICK KLUIVERT* -- 2004

10 *FABIAN SCHÄR* -- 2018

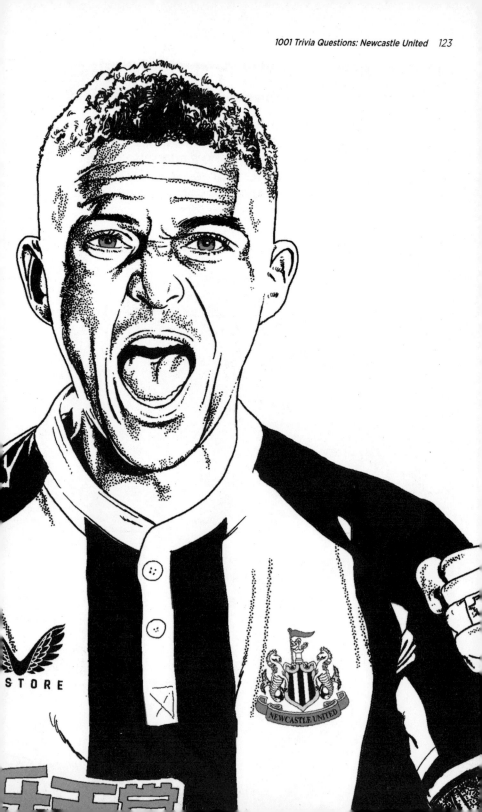

THE BHOYS

SCOTLAND CAPTAIN *ROY AITKEN* WON SIX LEAGUE TITLES AND SIX DOMESTIC CUPS WITH *CELTIC* BEFORE JOINING *NEWCASTLE* IN 1990. HE LATER MANAGED *ABERDEEN*, STEERING *"THE DONS"* TO A LEAGUE CUP FINAL WIN IN 1996. HE SUBSEQUENTLY COACHED WITH *LEEDS, ASTON VILLA* AND *BIRMINGHAM CITY* AND AS FAR AFIELD AS THE MALDIVES AND DUBAI.

IDENTIFY THESE OTHERS WHO PLAYED FOR *NEWCASTLE* AND *CELTIC*:

1 GOALKEEPER WHOSE OTHER CLUBS INCLUDED *BLACKBURN, SWINDON, SUNDERLAND, MANCHESTER CITY, ASTON VILLA, MIDDLESBROUGH* AND *STOKE.*

2 *CELTIC* AND *HIBERNIAN* DEFENDER WHO JOINED *NEWCASTLE* IN 1966 AND WON THE 1969 INTER-CITIES FAIRS CUP. HE WENT ON TO PLAY FOR *BLACKBURN, HARTLEPOOL UNITED* AND MORE.

3 *AUSTRALIA* STRIKER WHO PLAYED FOR *CELTIC, LEEDS UNITED* AND *MIDDLESBROUGH* BEFORE JOINING *NEWCASTLE* IN 2007.

4 GOALKEEPER WHO JOINED *CELTIC* FROM *NEWCASTLE* AND SET A SCOTTISH TOP DIVISION RECORD OF 1,256 MINUTES WITHOUT CONCEDING A GOAL. AN *ENGLAND* INTERNATIONAL, HE SIGNED FOR *SOUTHAMPTON* IN 2014, ALTHOUGH HE SUBSEQUENTLY RETURNED TO *"THE BHOYS"* ON LOAN.

5 MIDFIELDER WHO LEFT *NEWCASTLE* IN 1993 AND WON TWO PROMOTIONS WITH *BOLTON WANDERERS* BEFORE JOINING *ASTON VILLA* IN 1998. HE MOVED ON TO *CELTIC* IN 2000, WHERE HE WON MULTIPLE HONOURS AND REACHED THE UEFA CUP FINAL -- AND WON HIS SOLITARY *ENGLAND* CAP -- BEFORE SIGNING FOR *LEEDS UNITED* IN 2007.

6 *WALES* INTERNATIONAL WHO HAD TWO SPELLS AT *LIVERPOOL,* TWO AT *CARDIFF CITY,* PLAYED FOR *MANCHESTER CITY, WEST HAM, BLACKBURN* AND MORE. HE WON THE 2005 SCOTTISH CUP WITH *CELTIC* WHILE IN LOAN FROM *NEWCASTLE.*

7 *SCOTLAND* STRIKER WHO HAD TWO SPELLS AT *NEWCASTLE,* EITHER SIDE OF SPELLS WITH *ABERDEEN, CELTIC* AND *HAMBURGER SV.*

THE DRAGONS

IAN RUSH MADE HIS DEBUT FOR *WALES* BEFORE HE HAD EVEN BEEN HANDED HIS FIRST START FOR *LIVERPOOL.* IN 73 APPEARANCES FOR *"THE DRAGONS"* HE FOUND THE NET 28 TIMES, A GOALSCORING RECORD THAT STOOD FOR 12 YEARS UNTIL IT WAS SURPASSED BY *GARETH BALE.*

IDENTIFY THESE OTHER *NEWCASTLE* PLAYERS CAPPED BY *WALES:*

1 85 CAPS: WON MULTIPLE HONOURS WITH *LEEDS UNITED* AND LATER MANAGED THE *WALES* TEAM, HE DIED IN TRAGIC CIRCUMSTANCES IN 2011.

2 78 CAPS: 2007 WELSH FOOTBALLER OF THE YEAR, HE NEVER WON A PREMIER LEAGUE DESPITE PLAYING FOR FOUR TEAMS THAT WON THE TITLE.

3 68 CAPS: THE "GOLDEN BOY OF WELSH FOOTBALL", A £28,000 SIGNING TO *NEWCASTLE* IN 1958, HE WON WELSH CUPS WITH *SWANSEA TOWN* AND *CARDIFF CITY.*

4 34 CAPS: PLAYED FOR BOTH MANCHESTER CLUBS, *BOLTON* AND MORE, 1969 INTER-CITIES FAIRS CUP-WINNER WITH *NEWCASTLE.*

5 23 CAPS: HAVING WON HONOURS WITH *CARDIFF CITY* AND *SWINDON TOWN,* HE PLAYED FOR *NEWCASTLE* ON LOAN FROM *CRYSTAL PALACE* IN 1991. SUBSEQUENTLY *WALES U-21* COACH.

6 18 CAPS: LONG-SERVING VETERAN OF THE *WIMBLEDON* "CRAZY GANG", HE SIGNED FOR *NEWCASTLE* IN 1987 BUT WAS SOON REUNITED WITH *"THE DONS"* MANAGER *DAVE BASSETT* AT *WATFORD.* THE PAIR SUBSEQUENTLY WORKED TOGETHER AGAIN AT *SHEFFIELD UNITED* AND *NOTTINGHAM FOREST.* HE WAS APPOINTED MANAGER OF *AFC WIMBLEDON* IN 2019.

7 14 CAPS: FORMER *WATFORD, ASTON VILLA, NORWICH* AND *MILLWALL* STRIKER WHO JOINED *NEWCASTLE* IN 1993, WHERE HE SUFFERED THE SERIOUS ANKLE INJURY THAT ULTIMATELY ENDED HIS PLAYING CAREER.

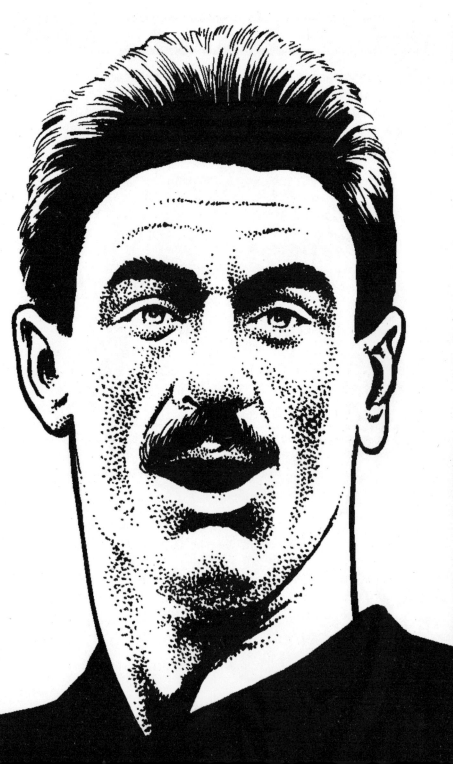

BACK IN MY DAY

OSSIE ARDILES BEGAN HIS MANAGEMENT CAREER IN ENGLAND, COACHING ***SWINDON TOWN, NEWCASTLE*** -- WHERE HE BECAME THE CLUB'S FIRST-EVER FOREIGN MANGER -- AND ***WEST BROMWICH ALBION***, BEFORE RETURNING TO FORMER CLUB ***SPURS*** TO BECOME THE FIRST PREMIER LEAGUE MANAGER FROM ARGENTINA.

ARDILES WAS A MEMBER OF THE **ARGENTINA** TEAM THAT WON THE WORLD CUP IN 1978 AND WON NUMEROUS HONOURS AT **TOTTENHAM**, INCLUDING THE UEFA CUP AND TWO FA CUPS.

WHICH **NEWCASTLE** MANAGER'S HONOURS DURING HIS PLAYING DAYS INCLUDE THE FOLLOWING?

1   THREE EUROPEAN CUPS, FIVE LEAGUE TITLES IN ENGLAND, A LEAGUE TITLE IN SCOTLAND, A COPPA ITALIA AND MORE?

2   THREE PREMIER LEAGUE TITLES, THREE FA CUPS, THE EUROPEAN CUP WINNERS' CUP, LEAGUE CUPS WITH TWO TEAMS AND MORE?

3   A UEFA EUROPEAN CHAMPIONSHIP, TWO EUROPEAN CUPS, THREE SERIE A TITLES, EREDIVISIE TITLES WITH TWO TEAMS AND MORE?

4   THE FA CUP, TWO LEAGUE CUPS AND THE UEFA CUP WITH **TOTTENHAM**?

5   PROMOTIONS WITH **BOLTON WANDERERS** AND **PRESTON NORTH END**.

6   A LEAGUE TITLE, THE FA CUP, THE LEAGUE CUP, TWO INTER-CITIES FAIRS CUPS AND THE WORLD CUP?

7   THREE EUROPEAN CUPS, SIX LEAGUE TITLES, FOUR LEAGUE CUPS, THE FA CUP, FOUR SCOTTISH LEAGUE TITLES, FOUR SCOTTISH CUPS AND A SCOTTISH LEAGUE CUP?

8   TWO FA CUPS AND THE UEFA CUP WITH **SPURS** AND A THIRD DIVISION TITLE WITH **BRENTFORD**?

9   PROMOTIONS WITH TWO CLUBS AND THE 1991 LEAGUE CUP?

10   A EUROPEAN CUP, TWO UEFA CUPS, THREE LEAGUE TITLES, THE FA CUP AND A BUNDESLIGA LEAGUE TITLE?

11   THE 1995 PREMIER LEAGUE?

COCKERELS OF THE NORTHEAST

PFA YOUNG PLAYER OF THE YEAR *PAUL GASCOIGNE* JOINED *SPURS* FOR A BRITISH RECORD FEE OF £2.2 MILLION IN JULY, 1988. THE NEWS CAME AS A SURPRISE TO *MANCHESTER UNITED* BOSS *ALEX FERGUSON*, WHO HAD GONE ON HOLIDAY TO MALTA AFTER RECEIVING ASSURANCES FROM *GAZZA* THAT HE WOULD BE SIGNING FOR *UNITED*.

NAME THESE OTHERS WHO PLAYED FOR *NEWCASTLE* AND *TOTTENHAM*:

1   HAVING JOINED *SPURS* AT THE AGE OF EIGHT, HE SPENT 16 YEARS WITH THE CLUB, DURING WHICH TIME HE WAS LOANED OUT TO NINE TEAMS -- INCLUDING *BIRMINGHAM CITY* AND *QPR* -- BEFORE JOINING *NEWCASTLE* IN A £12 MILLION DEAL IN EARLY 2016. HE JOINED *CRYSTAL PALACE* A FEW MONTHS LATER, STAYING AT *SELHURST PARK* FOR FIVE YEARS BEFORE MOVING TO *EVERTON*.

2   FRENCH DEFENDER CAPPED 15 TIMES BY *CAMEROON*, HIS ONE SEASON AT *NEWCASTLE* SAW HIM NAMED THE CLUB'S PLAYER OF THE YEAR, DESPITE TWO RED CARDS AND INJURY. FOLLOWING RELEGATION, HE PUSHED FOR HIS £8 MILLION MOVE TO *SPURS* IN 2009 AND LATER PLAYED FOR *NORWICH, WATFORD* AND *WOLVES*.

3   *ENGLAND* LEFT-BACK WHO BROKE THROUGH AT *LEEDS*. HE SPENT 13 SEASONS AT *TOTTENHAM* -- DURING WHICH HE WAS LOANED OUT TO A NUMBER OF CLUBS, INCLUDING *SUNDERLAND* AND *NEWCASTLE* -- BEFORE JOINING *WATFORD* IN 2021.

4   *REPUBLIC OF IRELAND* RIGHT-BACK WHO WON THE 1999 LEAGUE CUP IN HIS 11 SEASONS WITH *SPURS*, THE UEFA INTERTOTO CUP IN HIS FOUR SEASONS WITH *NEWCASTLE*, AND THE 2011 LEAGUE CUP WITH *BIRMINGHAM CITY*.

5   *UNITED STATES* RIGHT-BACK, JOINED *NEWCASTLE* FROM *SPURS* IN 2016 AND MOVED TO *GALATASARAY* IN 2021.

6   SPEEDY, TRICKY WINGER WHO MADE HIS REPUTATION AT *NORWICH* BEFORE JOINING *NEWCASTLE* IN A £2,250,000 DEAL IN 1994. A £4.5 MILLION SIGNING TO *SPURS* 18 MONTHS LATER, HE ENDED HIS LEAGUE CAREER AT *WEST BROM*.

7   *FRANCE* MIDFIELDER WHO CAPTAINED THE *NEWCASTLE* SIDE THAT FAILED TO BEAT THE DROP IN 2016, AFTER WHICH HE WAS SOLD TO *SPURS* IN A £30 MILLION DEAL. HE JOINED *WATFORD* IN 2021.

RECORD SETTERS

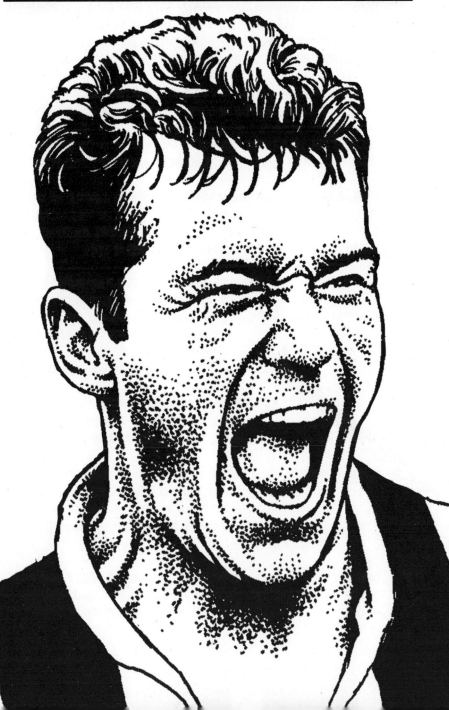

IN JANUARY, 2003, **ALAN SHEARER** TOOK JUST 10.4 SECONDS TO FIND THE NET IN A PREMIER LEAGUE GAME AGAINST **MANCHESTER CITY**, SETTING A NEW RECORD FOR **NEWCASTLE'S** FASTEST RECORDED GOAL.

IDENTIFY THESE OTHER RECORD-SETTING MILESTONES:

1 WHO WERE THE OPPONENTS WHEN **NEWCASTLE** RECORDED A RECORD 13-0 VICTORY IN THE OLD SECOND DIVISION IN 1946?

2 WHO BECAME **NEWCASTLE'S** OLDEST PLAYER WHEN HE TURNED OUT AGAINST **BIRMINGHAM CITY** IN A FIRST DIVISION GAME IN 1927 AT THE AGE OF 44 YEARS 225 DAYS?

3 WHO WAS THE FIRST **NEWCASTLE** PLAYER TO WIN THE PREMIER LEAGUE GOLDEN BOOT?

4 TO DATE, WHO IS THE ONLY **NEWCASTLE** BOSS TO WIN PREMIER LEAGUE MANAGER OF THE SEASON, WINNING IN 2012?

5 WHO HANDED OUT **NEWCASTLE'S** RECORD LOSS, A 9-0 THRASHING IN APRIL, 1895?

6 WHO HOLDS THE **NEWCASTLE** APPEARANCE RECORD OF 496 GAMES, SET BETWEEN 1904 AND 1922?

7 **NEWCASTLE'S** FIRST APPEARANCE IN THE UEFA CHAMPIONS LEAGUE CAME IN THE 1997-98 SEASON AND BROUGHT A 3-2 HOME VICTORY OVER **BARCELONA**. **LUIS ENRIQUE** AND **FIGO** SCORED FOR THE VISITORS -- BUT WHO HIT A HAT-TRICK FOR **"THE MAGPIES"**?

8 WHO WAS THE FIRST **NEWCASTLE** MANAGER BORN OUTSIDE THE BRITISH ISLES?

PAVEL IS A GEORDIE

AFTER ARRIVING ON TYNESIDE IN EARLY 1991, **PAVEL SRNÍČEK** STRUGGLED WITH THE LANGUAGE AND ADJUSTING TO THE ENGLISH GAME. AFTER A ROCKY START TO HIS **NEWCASTLE** CAREER, HE EVENTUALLY FOUND HIS BEST FORM WHEN **KEVIN KEEGAN** REPLACED **OSSIE ARDILES**. THE **CZECH REPUBLIC** GOALKEEPER'S WARM RELATIONSHIP WITH THE FANS WAS CEMENTED WHEN, DURING A LAP OF HONOUR FOLLOWING A 7-1 THRASHING OF **LEICESTER CITY**, HE PULLED UP HIS JERSEY TO REVEAL A T-SHIRT BEARING THE INSCRIPTION **"PAVEL IS A GEORDIE"**. AFTER LEAVING THE CLUB IN 1998, HE PLAYED FOR A NUMBER OF TEAMS -- INCLUDING **SHEFFIELD WEDNESDAY** AND **WEST HAM** -- BEFORE ENDING HIS PLAYING CAREER BACK AT **NEWCASTLE** IN THE 2006-07 SEASON AS COVER FOR **SHAY GIVEN**. IN 2015, WHILE OUT JOGGING -- AND WEARING THE SHIRT OF HIS BELOVED **NEWCASTLE** -- THE 47-YEAR-OLD COLLAPSED. AS HE LAY IN A COMA IN AN OSTRAVA HOSPITAL, HIS FAMILY PLAYED HIM RECORDINGS OF **NEWCASTLE** FANS SINGING **"PAVEL IS A GEORDIE"**. SADLY, IT WAS TO NO AVAIL AND HE WAS PRONOUNCED DEAD ON DECEMBER 29, 2015.

PAVEL WAS CAPPED 49 TIMES BY THE **CZECH REPUBLIC**. WHICH COUNTRY DID THE FOLLOWING NEWCASTLE PLAYERS REPRESENT?

1 HARIS VUČKIĆ

2 TAMÁS KÁDÁR

3 BJARNI GUÐJÓNSSON

4 SHEFKI KUQI

5 DAVID ROZEHNAL

6 TEMUR KETSBAIA

7 MARTIN DÚBRAVKA

8 EMIL KRAFTH

9 FABIAN SCHÄR

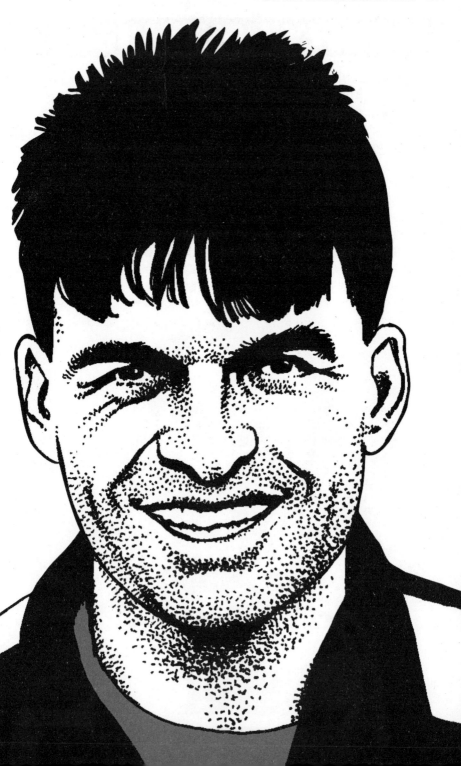

HARVEY BALLBANGER

NEWCASTLE UNITED WON THE FA CUP THREE YEARS OUT OF FIVE IN THE 1950S, BEATING **BLACKPOOL** 2-0 IN 1951 ... **ARSENAL** 1-0 IN 1952 ... AND **MANCHESTER CITY** 3-1 IN 1955.

JOE HARVEY CAPTAINED THE TEAM IN THE FIRST TWO OF THOSE VICTORIES. **NEWCASTLE'S** LONGEST-SERVING CAPTAIN, HE WENT ON TO MANAGE THE CLUB BETWEEN 1962 AND 1975, WINNING A SECOND DIVISION TITLE AND THE 1969 FAIRS CUP.

HARVEY ENDED HIS PLAYING DAYS AT **NEWCASTLE**, RETIRING IN 1953 AT THE AGE OF 34 WHILE STILL A FIRST TEAM REGULAR. WHICH TEAM DID THE FOLLOWING FA CUP WINNERS JOIN NEXT?

1   *BOBBY CORBETT*

2   *ERNIE TAYLOR*

3   *JACKIE MILBURN*

4   *BOB STOKOE*

5   *GEORGE HANNAH*

6   *RON BATTY*

7   *TOMMY CASEY*

8   *LEN WHITE*

9   *VIC KEEBLE*

10 *JIMMY SCOULAR*

"LIFE IS SO GOOD IN AMERICA ..."

WHEN **RUUD GULLIT** WAS APPOINTED HEAD COACH OF THE **LOS ANGELES GALAXY** IN LATE 2007, SIGNING A THREE-YEAR CONTRACT, HIS US$2 MILLION PER YEAR SALARY WAS THE HIGHEST EVER GIVEN TO A MAJOR LEAGUE SOCCER HEAD COACH !

WITH WHICH NORTH AMERICAN CLUB DID THE FOLLOWING PLAY?

1 **PETER BEARDSLEY:**
A) **CF MONTRÉAL**
B) **TORONTO FC** OR
C) **VANCOUVER WHITECAPS**

2 **STEVE HOWEY:**
A) **NEW ENGLAND REVOLUTION**
B) **CHICAGO FIRE** OR
C) **PHILADELPHIA UNION**

3 **MIGUEL ALMIRÓN:**
A) **ATLANTA UNITED**
B) **AUSTIN FC** OR
C) **MINNESOTA UNITED**

4 **IMRE VARADI:**
A) **NEW YORK COSMOS**
B) **SOUTH JERSEY BARONS** OR
C) **INTER MIAMI**

5 **GABRIEL OBERTAN:**
A) **CHATTANOOGA RED WOLVES**
B) **CHARLOTTE INDEPENDENCE** OR
C) **RICHMOND KICKERS**

6 **GIUSEPPE ROSSI:**
A) **REAL SALT LAKE**
B) **SAN JOSE EARTHQUAKES** OR
C) **PORTLAND TIMBERS**

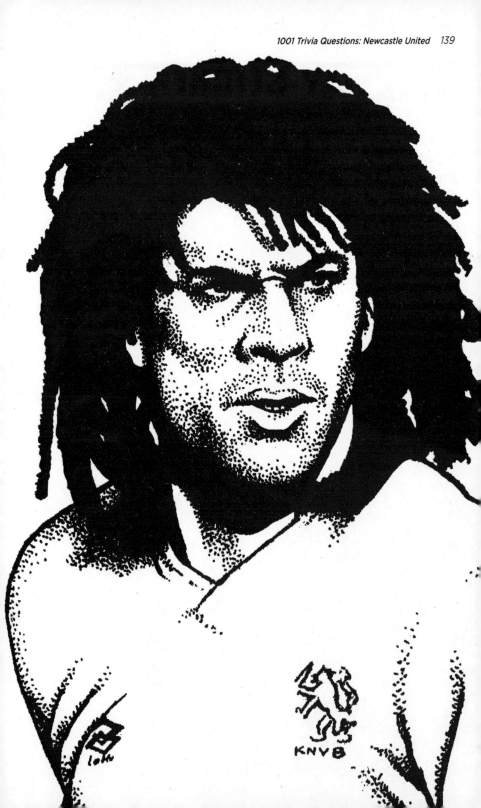

CITY SLICKERS

HAVING MADE 462 APPEARANCES FOR *NEWCASTLE*, *REPUBLIC OF IRELAND* GOALKEEPER *SHAY GIVEN* JOINED *MANCHESTER CITY* IN EARLY 2009 IN A £6 MILLION DEAL.

IDENTIFY THESE OTHERS WHO PLAYED FOR BOTH *NEWCASTLE* AND *MANCHESTER CITY*:

1 MAGNET FOR MAYHEM THROUGHOUT A CAREER THAT TOOK HIM FROM *MANCHESTER CITY* TO *BURNLEY,* VIA *NEWCASTLE, QPR, MARSEILLE* AND *RANGERS* AND SUBSEQUENTLY INTO MANAGEMENT WITH *FLEETWOOD TOWN.*

2 FRENCH RIGHT-BACK SIGNED TO *NEWCASTLE* FROM *CANNES* IN 1998 FOLLOWING A LOAN SPELL AT *CHELSEA,* HE PLAYED IN THE 1999 FA CUP FINAL. HE JOINED *MANCHESTER CITY* IN 2000.

3 RIGHT-BACK WHO REACHED THE 1981 FA CUP FINAL WITH *MANCHESTER CITY,* HE WENT ON TO PLAY FOR *BIRMINGHAM* AND *NEWCASTLE,* THEN REJOINED *CITY* IN 1993 BEFORE ENDING HIS PLAYING DAYS WITH *BURNLEY.*

4 TALL FRENCH MIDFIELDER OF POLISH DESCENT, HE JOINED *NEWCASTLE* FROM *CITY* ON TRANSFER DEADLINE DAY IN 2006. HE LATER PLAYED FOR *WIGAN ATHLETIC* AND *NORWICH CITY.*

5 HAVING ESTABLISHED HIS GOALSCORING CREDENTIALS WITH *BOLTON WANDERERS, WALES* STRIKER WHO WON THE 1969 INTER-CITIES FAIRS CUP WITH *NEWCASTLE* BEFORE PLAYING FOR BOTH *MANCHESTER* CLUBS, *BLACKPOOL* AND A HANDFUL OF LOWER LEAGUE TEAMS.

6 CAPPED 14 TIMES BY *ENGLAND,* INSIDE-FORWARD WHO WON THE 1955 FA CUP WITH *NEWCASTLE* AND PLAYED FOR *SUNDERLAND, MANCHESTER CITY* AND *QUEEN OF THE SOUTH* IN A CAREER THAT INCLUDED TWO SPELLS WITH *CARLISLE UNITED.*

7 CENTRE-BACK WHO WON FIRST DIVISION TITLES WITH *NEWCASTLE* IN 1993 AND *MANCHESTER CITY* IN 2002, HE WAS CAPPED FOUR TIMES BY *ENGLAND.*

8 NOMADIC JAMAICAN STRIKER WHOSE CLUBS INCLUDED *LINCOLN CITY, BARNSLEY, SHEFFIELD WEDNESDAY, MANCHESTER CITY, NEWCASTLE, BLACKPOOL, BURY, BOLTON, ROTHERHAM UNITED* AND *DONCASTER ROVERS* AND MORE BETWEEN THE LATE 1970S AND EARLY 1990S.

BOBBY'S BOYS

EUROPEAN MANAGER OF THE YEAR IN 1996-97, SIR BOBBY ROBSON'S HONOURS INCLUDED THE UEFA CUP, THE EUROPEAN CUP WINNERS' CUP AND DOMESTIC HONOURS IN FOUR COUNTRIES.

AT WHICH CLUB DID HE MANAGE:

1 PEP GUARDIOLA

2 ALLAN CLARKE

3 RUSSELL LATAPY

4 RONALDO

5 RUUD VAN NISTELROOY

6 ROMÁRIO

7 JONATHAN WOODGATE

8 FERNANDO COUTO

9 ÉMERSON

10 ARNOLD MÜHREN

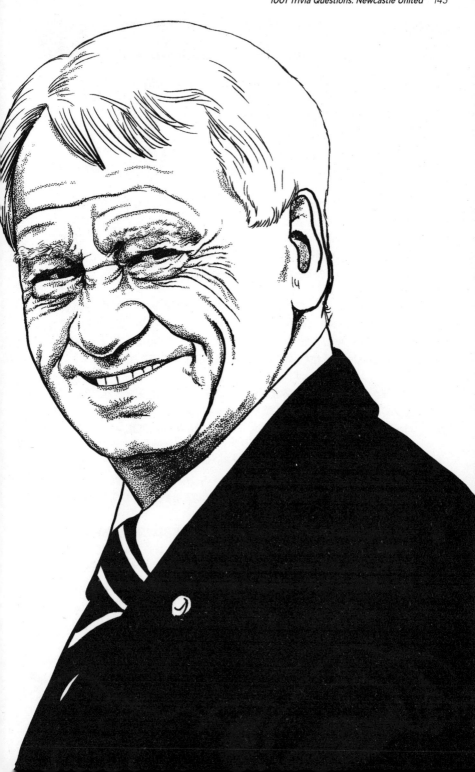

MAGPIE TROTTERS

IN A CAREER THAT SAW HIM PLAY FOR **LEEDS UNITED, EVERTON, NEWCASTLE, BOLTON WANDERERS** AND **SHEFFIELD UNITED,** MIDFIELDER **GARY SPEED** RACKED UP 535 PREMIER LEAGUE APPEARANCES, A RECORD THAT WAS LATER SURPASSED BY **DAVID JAMES.** CAPPED 85 TIMES BY **WALES, SPEED** WAS MANAGING THE NATIONAL TEAM AT THE TIME OF HIS DEATH IN 2011 AT THE AGE OF 42.

NAME THESE OTHERS WHO PLAYED FOR **BOLTON** AND **NEWCASTLE:**

1 SIGNED FROM **BOLTON** IN 1963, CENTRE-FORWARD WHO SCORED 46 GOALS IN 132 GAMES FOR **"THE MAGPIES"** BEFORE JOINING **BARROW.** HE LATER MANAGED **GATESHEAD.**

2 **SENEGAL** INTERNATIONAL DEFENDER WHO PLAYED UNDER **SAM ALLARDYCE** AT THREE CLUBS -- INCLUDING **NEWCASTLE** AND **BOLTON** -- AND HAD SPELLS AT **STOKE CITY** AND **HULL CITY** BEFORE JOINING MALAYSIA'S **SABAH FA** IN LATE 2014.

3 CAPPED 34 TIMES BY **WALES,** CENTRE-FORWARD WHO PLAYED FOR **BOLTON** AND **NEWCASTLE** IN THE 1960S, BEFORE GOING ON TO PLAY FOR BOTH MANCHESTER CLUBS, **BLACKPOOL** AND MORE.

4 BROTHER OF **SHOLA,** HE CAME THROUGH THE YOUTH RANKS AT **NEWCASTLE** BEFORE PLAYING FOR **BOLTON, CARDIFF CITY** AND **NOTTINGHAM FOREST.** HE JOINED **MIDDLESBROUGH** IN 2021.

5 FOLLOWING A LENGTHY STINT WITH **BLACKBURN ROVERS,** EITHER SIDE OF TWO SPELLS AT **LEEDS,** HE JOINED **NEWCASTLE** IN 1993, **BOLTON** IN 1995 AND LATER PLAYED FOR **HUDDERSFIELD, MANSFIELD TOWN** AND IN DENMARK WITH **AGF AARHUS.**

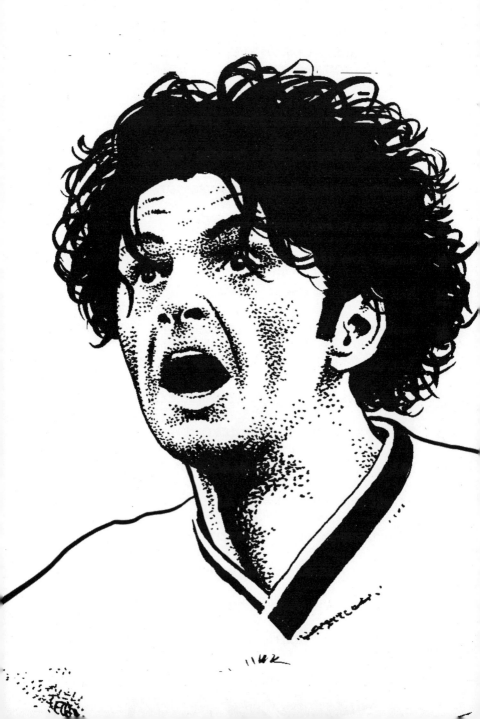

RAFA'S RECRUITS

THE REPORTED £21 MILLION TRANSFER FEE *RAFA BENITEZ* PAID TO BRING PARAGUAYAN *MIGUEL ALMIRÓN* TO *NEWCASTLE* FROM *ATLANTA UNITED* IN EARLY 2019 WAS NOT ONLY A CLUB RECORD, IT WAS THE HIGHEST FEE EVER PAID FOR AN MLS PLAYER.

IDENTIFY THESE OTHER PLAYERS SIGNED DURING THE *BENITEZ* TENURE:

1 JULY, 2016: £10 MILLION FROM *CRYSTAL PALACE*

2 JULY, 2016: £12 MILLION FROM *BOURNEMOUTH*

3 JULY, 2017: £10 MILLION FROM *NORWICH*

4 AUGUST, 2018: £9.5 MILLION FROM *1. FSV MAINZ 05*

5 JULY, 2017: £8.7 MILLION FROM *SD EIBAR*

6 AUGUST, 2016: £6 MILLION FROM *CHELSEA*

7 JULY, 2017: £7 MILLION FROM *BORUSSIA DORTMUND*

8 AUGUST, 2018: £6 MILLION FROM *SWANSEA CITY*

9 JUNE, 2016: £6.5 MILLION FROM *GENT*

10 JULY, 2016: £5.1 MILLION FROM *BLACKBURN ROVERS*

11 AUGUST, 2016: £5 MILLION FROM *ASTON VILLA*

12 AUGUST, 2016: £5 MILLION FROM *TOTTENHAM HOTSPUR*

13 AUGUST, 2017: £5 MILLION FROM *STOKE CITY*

14 AUGUST, 2016: £4.5 MILLION FROM *HULL CITY*

15 JULY, 2017: £4.5 MILLION FROM *ATLÉTICO MADRID*

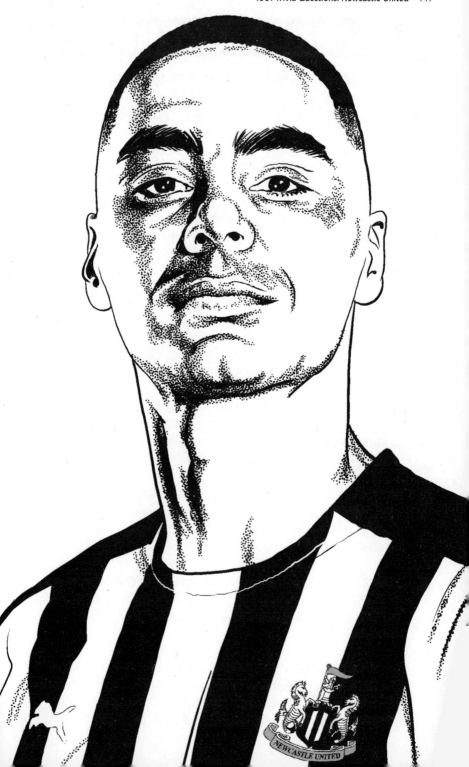

WILD ROVERS

ALAN SHEARER'S FOUR SEASONS AT **BLACKBURN ROVERS** SAW HIM WIN THE PREMIER LEAGUE TITLE IN 1996, WIN THE FIRST TWO OF HIS THREE CONSECUTIVE PREMIER LEAGUE GOLDEN BOOTS AND EARN PFA AND FWA PLAYER OF THE YEAR AWARDS.

IDENTIFY THESE OTHERS WHO PLAYED FOR **NEWCASTLE** AND **BLACKBURN ROVERS**:

1 A FIRST DIVISION WINNER WITH **NEWCASTLE**, HE WON FIVE PREMIER LEAGUE TITLES, TWO FA CUPS AND THE UEFA CHAMPIONS LEAGUE WITH **MANCHESTER UNITED** AND THE LEAGUE CUP WITH **BLACKBURN ROVERS**.

2 AFTER WINNING THE SCOTTISH LEAGUE DURING A LOAN SPELL WITH **CELTIC**, HE LEFT **NEWCASTLE** FOR **BLACKBURN ROVERS** IN 2005, WHERE HE WAS REUNITED WITH HIS FORMER **WALES** MANAGER, **MARK HUGHES**. THE TWO WOULD LATER WORK TOGETHER AGAIN AT **MANCHESTER CITY**.

3 CAPPED 92 TIMES BY **GEORGIA**, HE WON A SCOTTISH LEAGUE AND LEAGUE CUP DOUBLE WITH **RANGERS** AND LATER SPENT TIME ON LOAN AT **NEWCASTLE** IN LATE 2009 DURING HIS SIX SEASONS AT **EWOOD PARK**.

4 WHEN THE CENTRE-BACK SIGNED TO **NEWCASTLE** FROM **QPR** IN 1994, THE £440,000 **HEREFORD** RECEIVED THANKS TO A SELL-ON CLAUSE WAS A NEW CLUB RECORD! HE MOVED ON TO **BLACKBURN ROVERS** IN 1998.

5 FORWARD CAPPED 53 TIMES BY **SCOTLAND**, HAVING WON HONOURS WITH **DUNDEE** HE PLAYED FOR **COVENTRY CITY** AND **BLACKBURN** BEFORE BECOMING **BOBBY ROBSON'S** FIRST SIGNING FOR **NEWCASTLE**.

6 EX-**MANCHESTER UNITED** RIGHT-BACK WHO SPENT A SEASON ON LOAN AT **BLACKBURN**, HE WON PROMOTIONS TO THE PREMIER LEAGUE WITH **SUNDERLAND**, **NEWCASTLE** AND **QPR**, BEFORE WINNING THE PREMIER LEAGUE WITH **LEICESTER CITY** IN 2016.

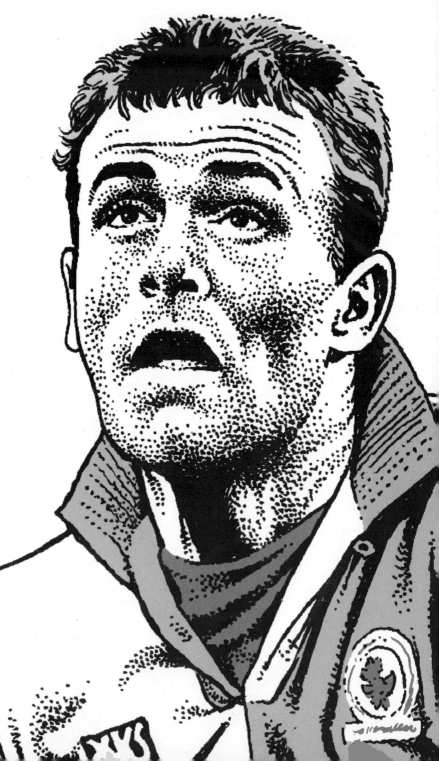

THE JOB CENTRE

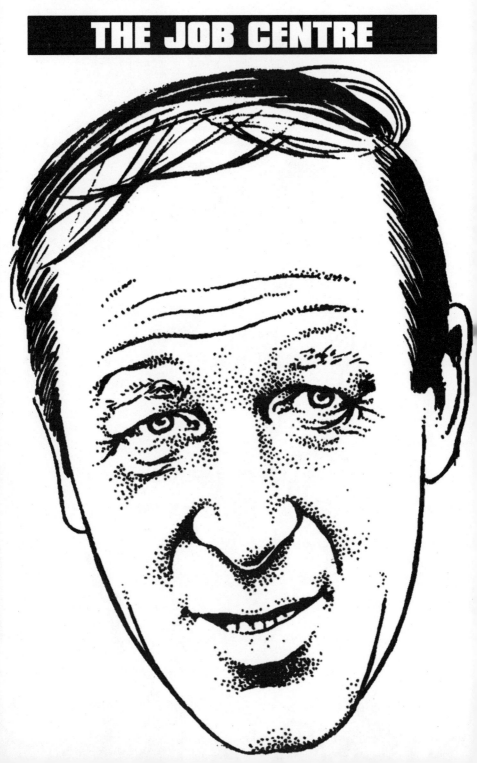

HAVING WON PROMOTIONS IN HIS TIME MANAGING *MIDDLESBROUGH* AND *SHEFFIELD WEDNESDAY*, A RELUCTANT *JACK CHARLTON* WAS PERSUADED TO TAKE THE *NEWCASTLE UNITED* JOB IN 1984 BY TYNESIDE LEGEND *JACKIE MILBURN*. *"BIG JACK"* EMPLOYED BASIC, ROUTE ONE TACTICS TO KEEP THE TEAM IN THE TOP FLIGHT BUT ALIENATED THE FANS IN THE PROCESS ... AND HE RESIGNED BEFORE THE START OF HIS SECOND SEASON. A FEW MONTHS LATER, HE ACCEPTED THE *REPUBLIC OF IRELAND* JOB, WHERE HE WOULD TAKE *"JACK'S ARMY"* TO UNPRECEDENTED LEVELS OF SUCCESS ON THE INTERNATIONAL STAGE.

JACK CHARLTON MANAGED BOTH *NEWCASTLE UNITED* AND *MIDDLESBROUGH*, AS DID *STEVE MCCLAREN*. NAME THE MEN WHO MANAGED (INCLUDING SPELLS AS CARETAKER OR INTERIM BOSS):

1   *NEWCASTLE* AND *BLACKBURN ROVERS* (5)

2   *NEWCASTLE* AND *CHELSEA* (2)

3   *NEWCASTLE* AND *BIRMINGHAM CITY* (3)

4   *NEWCASTLE* AND *SOUTHAMPTON* (3)

5   *NEWCASTLE* AND *SUNDERLAND* (2)

6   *NEWCASTLE* AND *NOTTINGHAM FOREST* (3)

7   *NEWCASTLE* AND *WEST BROMWICH ALBION* (4)

8   *NEWCASTLE* AND *QUEENS PARK RANGERS* (2)

9   *NEWCASTLE* AND *FULHAM* (2)

10   *NEWCASTLE* AND *LIVERPOOL* (3)

BOBBY'S BUYS

"A GREAT PLAYER WRAPPED ROUND AN UNUSUAL AND VOLATILE CHARACTER" WAS HOW *BOBBY ROBSON* DESCRIBED *CRAIG BELLAMY*, HIS £6.5 MILLION 2001 ACQUISITION FROM *COVENTRY CITY*. HIS SUBSEQUENT TIME AT THE CLUB WAS POCKMARKED WITH INJURIES AND DISCIPLINARY ISSUES AND IN EARLY 2005 HE WAS FARMED OUT TO *CELTIC* BY *ROBSON'S* EXASPERATED SUCCESSOR, *GRAEME SOUNESS*, BEFORE BEING SOLD TO **BLACKBURN ROVERS.**

IDENTIFY THESE OTHER PLAYERS SIGNED BY *BOBBY ROBSON* :

1   JULY, 2001: £9.5 MILLION FROM *PARIS SAINT-GERMAIN*

2   JANUARY, 2003: £9 MILLION FROM *LEEDS UNITED*

3   JUNE, 2002: £8.5 MILLION FROM *SPORTING CP*

4   JUNE, 2000: £7 MILLION FROM *WIMBLEDON*

5   FEBRUARY, 2002: £5 MILLION FROM *NOTTINGHAM FOREST*

6   JULY, 2004: £5 MILLION FROM *LEEDS UNITED*

7   JULY, 2002: £6 MILLION FROM *IPSWICH TOWN*

8   JUNE, 2000: £3.5 MILLION FROM *VÉLEZ SÁRSFIELD*

9   SEPTEMBER, 2000: £2.25 MILLION FROM *COLCHESTER UNITED*

10   JULY, 2004: £2.5 MILLION FROM *MANCHESTER UNITED*

11   MARCH, 2001: £2 MILLION FROM *BRADFORD CITY*

12   AUGUST, 2004: £2 MILLION FROM *TOTTENHAM HOTSPUR*

13   OCTOBER, 2000: £900,000 FROM *UNIVERSIDAD DE CHILE*

14   MARCH, 2003: £1 MILLION FROM *IPSWICH TOWN*

15   JULY, 2001: £800,000 FROM *SHEFFIELD UNITED*

16   AUGUST, 2004: £250,000 FROM *LE HAVRE*

17   JUNE, 2003: FREE TRANSFER FROM *WEST HAM UNITED*

18   JUNE, 2004: FREE TRANSFER FROM *BARCELONA*

19   JUNE, 2004: FREE TRANSFER FROM *ASTON VILLA*

20   JANUARY, 2004: FREE TRANSFER FROM *LEEDS UNITED*

SUR LE CONTINENT

ALTHOUGH THE PREMIER LEAGUE ATTRACTS TOP PLAYERS FROM EVERY CORNER OF THE GLOBE, IT IS STILL LESS COMMONPLACE TO SEE BRITISH PLAYERS, PARTICULARLY INTERNATIONAL STARS, MAKE A MOVE ABROAD.

THE LIKES OF *CHRIS WADDLE* -- WHO WON A FRENCH LEAGUE TITLE IN EACH OF HIS THREE SEASONS WITH *MARSEILLE* -- WAS AN EXCEPTION, RATHER THAN THE NORM. WITH WHICH CLUB DID THESE INTERNATIONAL STARS SPEND SOME TIME OUTSIDE OF BRITISH FOOTBALL?

1   *IAN RUSH* -- ITALY

2   *MICHAEL OWEN* -- SPAIN

3   *KEVIN KEEGAN* -- GERMANY

4   *PAUL GASCOIGNE* -- ITALY

5   *MARK MCGHEE* -- GERMANY

6   *JONATHAN WOODGATE* -- SPAIN

7   *JOEY BARTON* -- FRANCE

8   *KIERAN TRIPPIER* -- SPAIN

O BROTHER, WHERE ART THOU?

WHEN DUTCH ATTACKING MIDFIELDER *SIEM DE JONG* JOINED *NEWCASTLE* IN 2014, SIX MONTHS AFTER THE TEMPORARY ARRIVAL OF HIS BROTHER *LUUK*, THE PAIR WERE FOLLOWING IN THE FOOTSTEPS OF A NUMBER OF SIBLINGS WHO PLAYED FOR *NEWCASTLE* -- SOME AT THE SAME TIME*!*

IDENTIFY THESE *"MAGPIE"* BROTHERS:

1   *JORGE* AND *EDUARDO*

2   *RON* AND *CHRIS*

3   *ALAN* AND *KEITH*

4   *PETER* AND *CHRIS*

5   *STEVEN* AND *GARY*

6   *JAMIE* AND *STEVEN*

7   *LOMANA* AND *KAZENGA*

8   *SHOLA*, *TOMI* AND *SAMMY*

9   *SEAN* AND *MATTY*

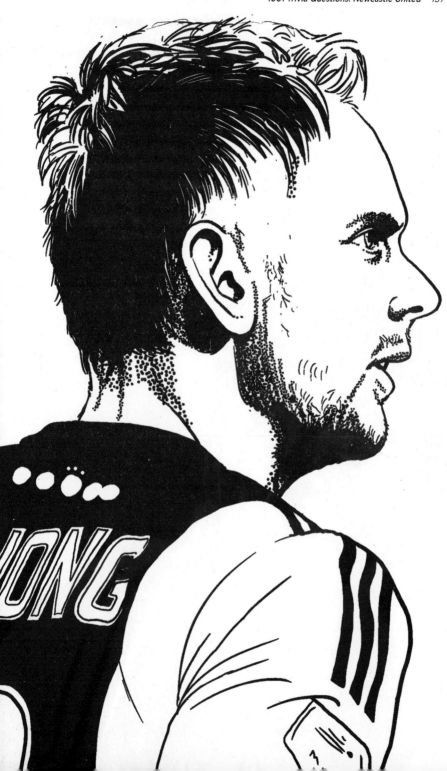

PAYING THEIR DUES 2

HAVING LAUNCHED HIS PLAYING CAREER WITH *GILLINGHAM,* *STEVE BRUCE* WON A SECOND DIVISION TITLE AND THE LEAGUE CUP DURING HIS THREE AND A HALF YEARS AT *NORWICH CITY.* HE WON A PLETHORA OF HONOURS WITH *MANCHESTER UNITED,* INCLUDING THREE LEAGUE TITLES, THREE FA CUPS, THE LEAGUE CUP, THE EUROPEAN CUP WINNERS' CUP AND THE EUROPEAN SUPER CUP BEFORE ENDING HIS PLAYING DAYS WITH SPELLS AT *BIRMINGHAM CITY* AND *SHEFFIELD UNITED.*

IDENTIFY THESE *NEWCASTLE UNITED* MANAGERS -- INCLUDING CARETAKER MANAGERS -- BY THE TEAMS THEY PLAYED FOR:

1 TOTTENHAM HOTSPUR, BRIGHTON & HOVE ALBION

2 HULL CITY, DERBY COUNTY, LINCOLN CITY, BRISTOL CITY, OXFORD UNITED

3 INSTITUTO DE CÓRDOBA, BELGRANO, HURACÁN, TOTTENHAM HOTSPUR, PARIS SAINT-GERMAIN, ST GEORGE FC, BLACKBURN ROVERS, QUEENS PARK RANGERS, FORT LAUDERDALE STRIKERS, SWINDON TOWN

4 SCUNTHORPE UNITED, LIVERPOOL, HAMBURGER SV, SOUTHAMPTON, BLACKTOWN CITY

5 SHEFFIELD UNITED, ALDERSHOT, HALIFAX TOWN, LINCOLN CITY, BOSTON UNITED, COLCHESTER UNITED

6 SHREWSBURY TOWN, SHEFFIELD WEDNESDAY, MIDDLESBROUGH

7 BOLTON WANDERERS, SUNDERLAND, MILLWALL, TAMPA BAY ROWDIES, COVENTRY CITY, HUDDERSFIELD TOWN, PRESTON NORTH END, WEST BROMWICH ALBION, LIMERICK

8 LEYTON ORIENT, QUEENS PARK RANGERS, NOTTS COUNTY, NEWCASTLE UNITED, WATFORD, GILLINGHAM

9 TOTTENHAM HOTSPUR, WEST HAM UNITED, BRENTFORD

10 HEDNESFORD TOWN, ASTON VILLA, SHREWSBURY TOWN

11 BURY, NEWCASTLE UNITED, LIVERPOOL, CORK CITY, APOEL

12 CELTIC, LIVERPOOL

13 PORT VALE, HUDDERSFIELD, BOURNEMOUTH & BOSCOMBE ATHLETIC

14 NORTH SHIELDS, BRIDLINGTON TOWN, DONCASTER ROVERS, WIGAN ATHLETIC, ST JOHNSTONE, SOUTHEND UNITED, BOSTON UNITED, BURY, CLYDE, HAMILTON ACADEMICAL

BRAVEHEARTS

BOBBY ROBSON'S FIRST SIGNING AS **NEWCASTLE** MANAGER, **KEVIN GALLACHER** PLAYED 53 TIMES FOR **SCOTLAND**, SCORING 9 GOALS. HE WAS PART OF THEIR EURO 92, EURO 96 AND WORLD CUP 98 SQUADS.

IDENTIFY THESE OTHER **NEWCASTLE** PLAYERS CAPPED BY **SCOTLAND**:

1 **NEWCASTLE** CAPTAIN SIGNED FROM **CELTIC** -- WITH WHOM HE WON SIX LEAGUE TITLES -- IN 1990. HE CAPTAINED **SCOTLAND** IN 27 OF HIS 57 APPEARANCES FOR HIS COUNTRY, INCLUDING PLAYING IN THE 1986 AND 1990 WORLD CUPS.

2 CAPTAIN OF **NEWCASTLE** IN THE LATE 1960S AND **SCOTLAND** IN THE EARLY 1970S, HE SCORED THREE GOALS ACROSS THE TWO LEGS OF THE FINAL WHEN **"THE MAGPIES"** WON THE INTER-CITIES FAIRS CUP IN 1969. CAPPED 16 TIMES.

3 PRIMARILY A WINGER, HE WON A LEAGUE CHAMPIONSHIP WITH **BOURNEMOUTH** IN 2015, BEFORE JOINING **NEWCASTLE** IN 2020. HE EARNED HIS FIRST CAP IN 2017 BUT DREW CRITICISM FOR MISSING A EURO 2020 QUALIFIER AGAINST **KAZAKHSTAN** AFTER DECLINING TO PLAY ON AN ARTIFICIAL SURFACE.

4 DEFENDER WHO EARNED HIS FIRST CAP IN 2011 WHILE WITH **BLACKBURN ROVERS**. A SUBSEQUENT CHAMPIONSHIP WINNER WITH **NEWCASTLE** IN 2017 AND **NORWICH CITY** IN 2019, HE PLAYED IN ALL THREE **SCOTLAND** GAMES AT EURO 2020.

5 ONE OF THE **"WEMBLEY WIZARDS"** WHO THRASHED ENGLAND 5-1 IN 1928, HE HIT 24 GOALS IN HIS 20 APPEARANCES FOR **SCOTLAND**.

6   ENGLAND-BORN WINGER WHO WON A PROMOTION WITH *SWINDON TOWN* IN 2012, *BOURNEMOUTH* IN 2015 AND *NEWCASTLE* IN 2017. NAMED SFWA PLAYER OF THE YEAR IN 2016, TWO YEARS LATER HE REQUESTED NOT TO BE CONSIDERED FOR FURTHER SELECTION.

7   LIKE HIS BROTHER *GARY*, A *SCOTLAND* INTERNATIONAL WHO CAME THROUGH THE RANKS AT *NEWCASTLE*. HE WON PROMOTIONS WITH *SUNDERLAND* AND *BURNLEY*, PLAYED FOR *WIGAN ATHLETIC* AND *BIRMINGHAM CITY* AND MOVED TO CANADA IN THE MID-2010S.

HAT-TRICK HEROICS

MICHAEL OWEN PLAYED FOR FOUR DIFFERENT TEAMS IN
THE PREMIER LEAGUE DURING HIS CAREER -- **LIVERPOOL,**
NEWCASTLE, MANCHESTER UNITED AND **STOKE CITY**
-- AND HIT EIGHT PREMIER LEAGUE HAT-TRICKS. HIS FIRST
CAME FOR **LIVERPOOL** AGAINST **SHEFFIELD WEDNESDAY**
IN 1998. AT JUST 18 YEARS AND 62 DAYS, **OWEN** WAS THE
YOUNGEST-EVER PLAYER TO HIT A PREMIER LEAGUE HAT-TRICK.
HIS LAST PREMIER LEAGUE HAT-TRICK WAS HIS ONLY TRIPLE FOR
NEWCASTLE, COMING IN A 4-2 WIN OVER **WEST HAM** IN 2005.

IDENTIFY THESE HAT-TRICK HEROES FOR **NEWCASTLE** IN THE
PREMIER LEAGUE:

1   OCTOBER 30, 1993: **WIMBLEDON** 4-0
THREE GOALS FOR A RETURNING HERO FOLLOWING HIS
SUMMER TRANSFER FROM **EVERTON**

2   NOVEMBER 21, 1993: **LIVERPOOL** 3-0
THE SEASON'S END WOULD SEE THE SCORER WIN THE GOLDEN
BOOT AND THE PFA YOUNG PLAYER OF THE YEAR AWARD

3   OCTOBER 21, 1995: **WIMBLEDON** 6-1
KEEGAN'S ENTERTAINERS SMASHED THE "CRAZY GANG" WHO HAD
VINNIE JONES IN GOAL AFTER GOALKEEPER **PAUL HEALD** WAS
DISMISSED FOR TWO YELLOW CARDS

4   SEPTEMBER 19, 1999: **SHEFFIELD WEDNESDAY** 8-0
FIVE-GOAL SPREE FROM THE FRONTMAN

5   AUGUST 22, 2010: **ASTON VILLA** 6-0
GIVEN THE ICONIC NUMBER 9 SHIRT FOR THE NEW SEASON, HE
WOULD CAPTAIN THE TEAM IN OCTOBER BUT BE GONE
TO MERSEYSIDE BEFORE THE END OF JANUARY

6   OCTOBER 31, 2010: **SUNDERLAND** 5-1
TITUS BRAMBLE WAS SENT OFF FOR
STEVE BRUCE'S SUNDERLAND

7 JANUARY 5, 2011: ***WEST HAM UNITED*** 5-0
THREE GOALS FROM ***REPUBLIC OF IRELAND*** STRIKER NICKNAMED
"ZORRO" AT PREVIOUS CLUB ***COVENTRY CITY***

8 SEPTEMBER 23, 2011: ***BLACKBURN ROVERS*** 3-1
FIRST HAT-TRICK IN ENGLISH FOOTBALL FOR SENEGALESE STRIKER

9 OCTOBER 18, 2015: ***NORWICH CITY*** 6-2
FOUR GOALS FROM DUTCH MIDFIELDER RECRUITED THAT SUMMER

10 APRIL 20, 2019: ***SOUTHAMPTON*** 3-1
THE SPANISH MIDFIELDER'S NEXT HAT-TRICK WOULD BE FOR
LEICESTER CITY FOLLOWING HIS £30 MILLION TRANSFER

BACK OF THE NET!

WHILE PLAYING FOR **SOUTHAMPTON, BLACKBURN ROVERS**
AND **NEWCASTLE, ALAN SHEARER** SCORED 30 GOALS IN HIS 63
APPEARANCES FOR **ENGLAND,** CAPTAINING THE TEAM 34 TIMES.

IDENTIFY THESE OTHER **NEWCASTLE** PLAYERS FROM THEIR **ENGLAND**
TALLY AND THE CLUBS THEY PLAYED FOR AT THE TIMES THEY WERE
SELECTED BY THEIR COUNTRY:

1   40 GOALS (1998-2008):
     LIVERPOOL, REAL MADRID, NEWCASTLE

2   21 GOALS (1972-1977):
     SOUTHAMPTON, MANCHESTER CITY

3   21 GOALS (1972-1982):
     LIVERPOOL, SV HAMBURGER, SOUTHAMPTON

4   11 GOALS (1983-1995):
     WATFORD, LIVERPOOL

5   10 GOALS (1948-1955):
     NEWCASTLE

6   10 GOALS (1988-1998):
     **TOTTENHAM HOTSPUR, LAZIO,
     RANGERS, MIDDLESBROUGH**

7   9 GOALS (1986-1996):
     NEWCASTLE, LIVERPOOL

8   8 GOALS (1951-1954):
     MANCHESTER CITY, NEWCASTLE

9   6 GOALS (1972-1975):
     NEWCASTLE

10   6 GOALS (1985-1991):
      NEWCASTLE, TOTTENHAM HOTSPUR, MARSEILLE

11   5 GOALS (1987-1999):
NOTTINGHAM FOREST,
WEST HAM UNITED

12   5 GOALS (1993-1998):
QPR, NEWCASTLE,
TOTTENHAM HOTSPUR

ICI C'EST PARIS

DURING HIS THREE-AND-A-HALF SEASONS WITH **PARIS SAINT-GERMAIN**, THE FLAMBOYANT **DAVID GINOLA** WON THE LEAGUE AND THREE DOMESTIC CUPS AND WAS NAMED FRENCH PLAYER OF THE YEAR. HE JOINED **NEWCASTLE** IN 1995, MOVING ON TO **SPURS** TWO YEARS LATER.

IDENTIFY THESE OTHERS WHO PLAYED FOR **NEWCASTLE** AND **PSG**:

1 LEFT-WINGER WITH A THUNDERBOLT SHOT WHO JOINED **NEWCASTLE** FROM **PSG** FOR £9.5 MILLION IN 2001. FOLLOWING A PUBLIC FALLING OUT WITH **GRAEME SOUNESS**, HE WAS LOANED OUT TO **PORTSMOUTH** BEFORE BEING SOLD TO **BENFICA**.

2 LEFT-BACK WHO HAD TWO SPELLS AT **PARIS SAINT-GERMAIN** EITHER SIDE OF A TWO-YEAR STAY AT **NEWCASTLE**, DURING WHICH TIME HE PLAYED IN THE 1999 FA CUP FINAL. HE SUBSEQUENTLY PLAYED FOR **LEEDS UNITED**, **ESPANYOL**, **OLYMPIACOS** AND **NEW ENGLAND REVOLUTION**.

3 HAVING PLAYED FOR **NEWCASTLE** ON LOAN FROM **PSG**, HE JOINED **MANCHESTER CITY** IN 2002, BEFORE MOVING ON TO **PORTSMOUTH**, **EVERTON** AND **BOURNEMOUTH**.

4 HAVING WON A LEAGUE AND CUP DOUBLE WITH *LILLE*, THE *FRANCE* INTERNATIONAL MIDFIELDER JOINED *NEWCASTLE* IN 2011. HE SUBSEQUENTLY EARNED HONOURS AT *PARIS SAINT-GERMAIN* BEFORE JOINING *CRYSTAL PALACE* IN 2015.

5 CAPPED 60 TIMES BY THE *CZECH REPUBLIC*, HE WON A BELGIAN LEAGUE AND CUP DOUBLE WITH *CLUB BRUGGE* AND A COUPE DE FRANCE WITH *PSG* BEFORE JOINING *NEWCASTLE* IN 2011. HE SUBSEQUENTLY WON HONOURS WITH *LAZIO* AND *LILLE*.

COX'S CAPTURES

ARTHUR COX WAS THE MANAGER WHO BROUGHT SUPERSTAR KEVIN KEEGAN TO NEWCASTLE. AT THE END OF HIS TWO SEASONS PLAYING ON TYNESIDE, KEEGAN LED THE TEAM BACK TO THE TOP FLIGHT. HAVING FORGED A STRONG BOND, COX AND KEEGAN SUBSEQUENTLY WORKED TOGETHER REGULARLY, COX ACTING AS MANAGER KEEGAN'S "RIGHT-HAND MAN" AT FULHAM AND MANCHESTER CITY AND WITH ENGLAND. KEEGAN HAD WANTED TO MAKE COX ASSISTANT MANAGER OF THE NATIONAL TEAM BUT THE REQUEST WAS REFUSED ON THE GROUNDS OF AGE AND THE 60-YEAR-OLD WAS ASSIGNED A COACHING ROLE. WHEN KEEGAN'S SUCCESSOR, SVEN-GÖRAN ERIKSSON, WAS SUBSEQUENTLY ALLOWED TO APPOINT 64-YEAR-OLD TORD GRIP AS HIS ASSISTANT, AN AGGRIEVED KEEGAN MADE HIS DISPLEASURE KNOWN.

IDENTIFY THESE ARTHUR COX ACQUISITIONS AT NEWCASTLE:

1 DECEMBER, 1980: £180,000 FROM LINCOLN CITY

2 DECEMBER, 1983: £125,000 FROM QUEENS PARK RANGERS

3 SEPTEMBER, 1983: £150,000 FROM VANCOUVER WHITECAPS

4 AUGUST, 1981: £100,000 FROM EVERTON

5 SEPTEMBER, 1982: £100,000 FROM LIVERPOOL

6 FEBRUARY, 1983: £50,000 FROM BRISTOL ROVERS

7 JUNE, 1982: FREE TRANSFER FROM PRESTON NORTH END

8 JUNE, 1982: FREE TRANSFER FROM TULSA ROUGHNECKS

9 AUGUST, 1982: FREE TRANSFER FROM SOUTHAMPTON

10 JULY, 1982: FREE TRANSFER FROM SUNDERLAND

11 DECEMBER, 1983: £100,000 FROM HUDDERSFIELD TOWN

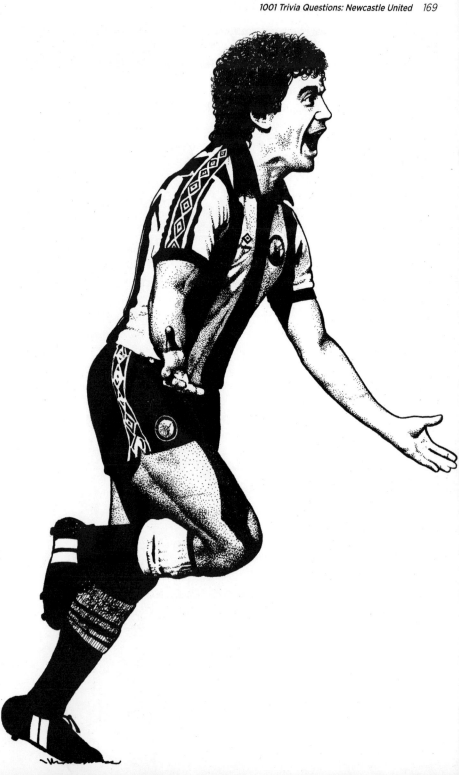

THE BOYS OF '76

NEWCASTLE REACHED THE LEAGUE CUP FINAL FOR THE FIRST TIME IN CLUB HISTORY -- AND SO FAR, THE ONLY TIME -- IN 1976. TEENAGE WINGER **PETER BARNES** GAVE OPPONENTS **MANCHESTER CITY** THE LEAD, BUT **ALAN GOWLING** EQUALISED FOR **GORDON LEE'S** TEAM. EARLY IN THE SECOND HALF, A SPECTACULAR OVERHEAD KICK FROM **DENNIS TUEART** -- A GEORDIE WHO HAD PREVIOUSLY PLAYED FOR **SUNDERLAND** -- WON THE GAME FOR THE SKY BLUES.

WHICH CLUBS DID THESE MEMBERS OF THAT 1976 LEAGUE CUP FINAL TEAM JOIN NEXT?

1 *MIKE MAHONEY*

2 *IRVING NATTRASS*

3 *ALAN KENNEDY*

4 *GLENN KEELEY*

5 *PAT HOWARD*

6 *STEWART BARROWCLOUGH*

7 *TOMMY CASSIDY*

8 *TOMMY CRAIG*

9 *MICKY BURNS*

10 *MALCOLM MACDONALD*

11 *ALAN GOWLING*

12 *PAUL CANNELL*

BRIGHT SPARKS

STUART PEARCE WORKED AS AN ELECTRICIAN WHILE PLAYING NON-LEAGUE FOOTBALL WITH **WEALDSTONE**. HE WAS 21 YEARS OLD WHEN HE TURNED PRO WITH **COVENTRY CITY**, GOING ON TO PLAY FOR **NOTTINGHAM FOREST**, **NEWCASTLE**, **WEST HAM** AND **MANCHESTER CITY** AND EARN 78 ENGLAND CAPS. HE SUBSEQUENTLY MANAGED **FOREST** AND **MANCHESTER CITY** AND **ENGLAND**, AT BOTH U-21 LEVEL AND AS CARETAKER OF THE SENIOR TEAM.

THE FOLLOWING **NEWCASTLE** PLAYERS ALL WENT INTO MANAGEMENT -- NAME ONE OF THE CLUBS THEY MANAGED:

1 MALCOLM MACDONALD

2 BOBBY MONCUR

3 DIETMAR HAMANN

4 BOB STOKOE

5 GEORGE EASTHAM

6 FRANK CLARK

7 PAUL BRACEWELL

8 GARY MEGSON

9 JIMMY SCOULAR

10 CHRIS WADDLE

11 POP ROBSON

12 JIM ILEY

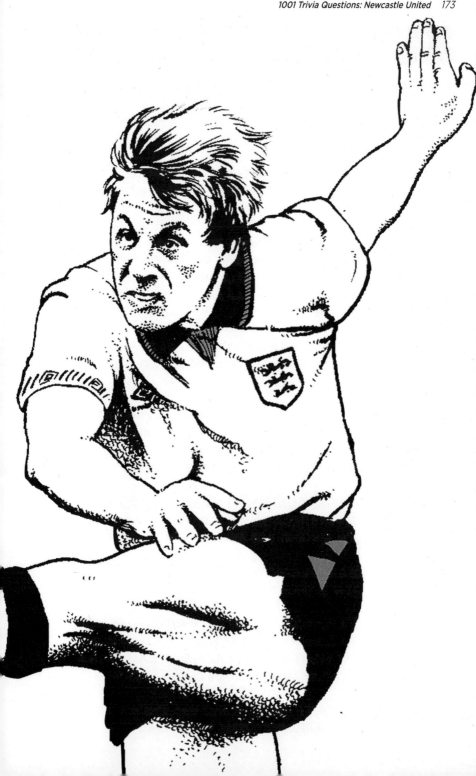

THE RUCKS

GIVEN THE TASK OF MAN-MARKING **PAUL GASCOIGNE** WHEN **WIMBLEDON** MET **NEWCASTLE** IN 1987, SELF-STYLED **"CRAZY GANG"** HARDMAN **VINNIE JONES** WAS PHOTOGRAPHED GRIPPING THE TEENAGER'S UNDERCARRIAGE.

1 WHICH TWO **NEWCASTLE UNITED** PLAYERS WERE RED-CARDED FOR FIGHTING EACH OTHER DURING A 2005 HOME GAME AGAINST **ASTON VILLA?**

2 WHILE PLAYING FOR **BLACKBURN**, JUST FOUR MINUTES INTO A 1995 CHAMPIONS LEAGUE CLASH WITH **SPARTAK MOSCOW**, A FIGHT BETWEEN **GRAEME LE SAUX** AND WHICH SUBSEQUENT **NEWCASTLE** MIDFIELDER LEFT **LE SAUX** WITH A BROKEN HAND AND A £12,000 FINE?

3 VIDEO EVIDENCE SHOWING A PUNCH TO THE RIBS OF **BLACKBURN'S MORTEN GAMST PEDERSEN** RESULTED IN A THREE-MATCH BAN IN 2010 FOR WHICH **NEWCASTLE** MIDFIELDER?

4 WHEN ONE WAS SENT OFF DURING THE GAME AND THE OTHER SUBSEQUENTLY CONVICTED ON VIDEO EVIDENCE, WHICH TWO **NEWCASTLE** PLAYERS SERVED BANS FOR VIOLENT CONDUCT AGAINST **BOLTON'S JOHAN ELMANDER** IN 2010?

5 WHILE PLAYING FOR **RANGERS**, A HEADBUTT ON **JOCK MCSTAY** OF **RAITH ROVERS** RESULTED IN A 12-GAME BAN AND A THREE-MONTH PRISON SENTENCE FOR WHICH EX-**NEWCASTLE** STRIKER?

6 **KEVIN KEEGAN** WAS SENT OFF FOR FIGHTING WITH WHICH **LEEDS UNITED** PLAYER IN THE 1974 CHARITY SHIELD GAME AT **WEMBLEY?**

7 IN LATE 1998, A HORROR TACKLE BY WHICH AUSTRALIAN HARDMAN -- NAMED BY A SPANISH WEBSITE AS FOOTBALL'S DIRTIEST-EVER PLAYER -- LEFT **NORWICH** WINGER **CRAIG BELLAMY** WITH A SERIOUS KNEE INJURY THAT RULED HIM OUT FOR MONTHS?

8 WHICH **MANCHESTER UNITED** PLAYER WAS SENT OFF FOR TRYING TO PUNCH **ALAN SHEARER** DURING A 2001 GAME?

9   IN 2013, A WILD CHALLENGE BY *WIGAN'S CALLUM MCMANAMAN* ON WHICH FRENCH FULL-BACK LED TO *NEWCASTLE* THREATENING TO SUE AND FORCED *THE FA* TO CHANGE ITS OWN LEGISLATION ON RETROACTIVE PUNISHMENT?

10   WHILE PLAYING FOR *EVERTON* IN 2006, WHICH FORMER *NEWCASTLE* STRIKER WAS BANNED FOR SEVEN GAMES -- THREE FOR A RED CARD FOR VIOLENT CONDUCT AFTER PUNCHING *WIGAN'S PAUL SCHARNER*, AND A FURTHER FOUR FOR PUSHING *PASCAL CHIMBONDA* IN THE FACE AFTER HIS SENDING OFF?

11   WHILE PLAYING FOR *QPR* IN 2012, WHO WAS BANNED FOR 12 GAMES FOR ELBOWING *CARLOS TEVEZ*, KNEEING *SERGIO AGÜERO* AND TRYING TO HEAD-BUTT *VINCENT KOMPANY* -- ALL WITHIN THE SPACE OF A MINUTE!

MARCHING ON TOGETHER

JAMES MILNER'S FIRST-TEAM DEBUT FOR *LEEDS UNITED* IN NOVEMBER OF 2002 MADE HIM THE SECOND-YOUNGEST PLAYER EVER TO PLAY IN THE PREMIER LEAGUE, AT THE AGE OF 16 YEARS AND 309 DAYS. A FEW WEEKS LATER, AT 16 YEARS AND 356 DAYS, HE BECAME THE YOUNGEST PLAYER TO THAT POINT TO SCORE IN THE PREMIER LEAGUE, WITH A GOAL IN A 2-1 VICTORY OVER SUNDERLAND.

IDENTIFY THESE OTHERS WHO PLAYED FOR *LEEDS* AND *NEWCASTLE*:

1 *ENGLAND* DEFENDER WHOSE PLAYING CAREER TOOK HIM FROM *LEEDS* TO *NEWCASTLE* AND THEN ON TO *REAL MADRID*, *MIDDLESBROUGH*, *SPURS* AND *STOKE*.

2 RACKED UP 841 APPEARANCES PLAYING FOR *LEEDS*, *EVERTON*, *NEWCASTLE*, *BOLTON* AND *SHEFFIELD UNITED* AND PLAYED FOR AND MANAGED *WALES*.

3 *AUSTRALIA* STRIKER WHO WON HONOURS WITH *DINAMO ZAGREB* AND *CELTIC* BEFORE PLAYING FOR *LEEDS*, *MIDDLESBROUGH* AND *NEWCASTLE*.

4 TOUGH-TACKLING *ENGLAND* MIDFIELDER WHO MADE MORE THAN 200 APPEARANCES FOR *LEEDS* BEFORE RELEGATION SAW HIM JOIN *MANCHESTER UNITED* IN 2004. HE WENT ON TO PLAY FOR *NEWCASTLE*, *MK DONS* AND *NOTTS COUNTY*.

5 HAVING WON MULTIPLE HONOURS WITH *AJAX*, MIDFIELDER WHO JOINED *NEWCASTLE* IN 2012. HAVING HELPED *NEWCASTLE* GAIN PROMOTION TO THE PREMIER LEAGUE IN 2017, HE JOINED *LEEDS* AND HAS SINCE PLAYED IN BULGARIA AND THE NETHERLANDS.

6 MIDFIELDER CAPPED 42 TIMES BY *ENGLAND*, HE WON TOP FLIGHT TITLES WITH *LEEDS* AND *BLACKBURN ROVERS* IN THE EARLY 1990S AND REACHED AN FA CUP FINAL IN HIS FOUR SEASONS WITH *NEWCASTLE*, BEFORE RETURNING TO *LEEDS* IN LATE 1998.

7 *WALES* SUPERSTAR WHO PLAYED FOR *LIVERPOOL*, *JUVENTUS*, *LEEDS*, *NEWCASTLE*, *SHEFFIELD UNITED* AND MORE.

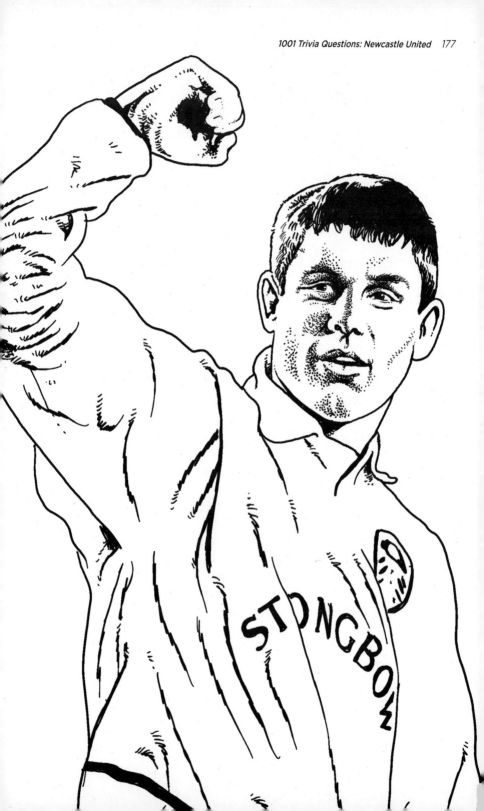

MEET THE NEW BOSS, SAME AS THE OLD BOSS

HAVING PLAYED UNDER **SAM ALLARDYCE** AT **NEWCASTLE**, **ANDY CARROLL** WAS REUNITED WITH **"BIG SAM"** AT **WEST HAM**.

AT WHICH CLUBS -- IN ADDITION TO **NEWCASTLE** -- DID THE FOLLOWING PLAYERS AND MANAGERS WORK TOGETHER?

1 *JOEY BARTON* AND MANAGER *KEVIN KEEGAN*

2 *LAURENT CHARVET* AND MANAGER *RUUD GULLIT*

3 *ANTOINE SIBIERSKI* AND MANAGER *GLENN ROEDER*

4 *DAVID BATTY* AND MANAGER *KENNY DALGLISH*

5 *ABDOULAYE FAYE* AND MANAGER *SAM ALLARDYCE*

6 *JOHN BARNES* AND MANAGER *KENNY DALGLISH*

7 *TIM KRUL* AND MANAGER *CHRIS HUGHTON*

8 *PETER BEARDSLEY* AND MANAGER *KEVIN KEEGAN*

9 *SHOLA AMEOBI* AND MANAGER *ALAN PARDEW*

10 *IAN RUSH* AND MANAGER *KENNY DALGLISH*

11 *KIERAN TRIPPIER* AND MANAGER *EDDIE HOWE*

12 *JONÁS GUTIÉRREZ* AND MANAGER *CHRIS HUGHTON*

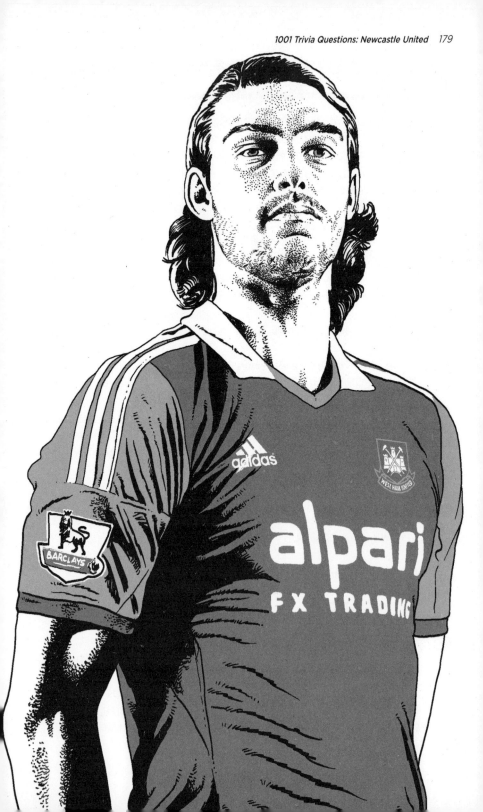

FALL OUT BOYS

ALAN *SHEARER* AND *MICHAEL OWEN* WERE A STRIKE PARTNERSHIP FOR *ENGLAND* AND *NEWCASTLE* AND GREAT FRIENDS OFF THE PITCH ... BUT THE RELATIONSHIP SOURED WHEN, IN AN EFFORT TO STAVE OFF IMPENDING RELEGATION, THE RECENTLY RETIRED *SHEARER* WAS INSTALLED AS *NEWCASTLE* MANAGER AT THE TAIL END OF THE 2008-09 SEASON. THE PERENNIALLY INJURED *OWEN* WAS ON THE MISSING LIST AS *NEWCASTLE* CRASHED OUT OF THE PREMIER LEAGUE. *SHEARER* MADE NO SECRET OF HIS BELIEF THAT *OWEN*, WITH ONE EYE ON THE EXIT, HAD DESERTED THE CLUB IN ITS TIME OF NEED. FOR HIS PART, *OWEN* HAS SAID HE BELIEVES HE WAS SCAPEGOATED. FUELLED BY SOCIAL MEDIA BARBS BETWEEN THE PAIR, THE FEUD HAS RUMBLED ON.

IDENTIFY THESE OTHER TYNESIDE TUSSLES:

1 WHICH RESERVE TEAM MANAGER, A FORMER *SCOTLAND* INTERNATIONAL, LEFT THE CLUB AFTER ALLEGATIONS THAT HE HAD LASHED OUT AT YOUNGSTER *REMIE STREETE?*

2 *CHARLES N'ZOGBIA* ANNOUNCED HE WOULD NO LONGER PLAY FOR THE CLUB AFTER WHICH MANAGER DUBBED HIM *"INSOMNIA"* DURING A TV INTERVIEW?

3 *HATEM BEN ARFA* WAS BANISHED TO THE RESERVES AND EVENTUALLY SHOWN THE DOOR AT *NEWCASTLE* AFTER CLASHING WITH WHICH MANAGER?

4 *CRAIG BELLAMY'S* FRACTIOUS RELATIONSHIP WITH WHICH MANAGER SAW THE *WALES* FORWARD FINED £80,000 AND FARMED OUT TO *CELTIC?*

5 *BELLAMY* WAS ONCE INVOLVED IN A PUNCH-SWINGING, CHAIR-THROWING AIRPORT BUST-UP WITH WHICH *NEWCASTLE* COACH?

6 *KEVIN KEEGAN'S* SECOND STINT AS *NEWCASTLE* BOSS ENDED AFTER DISAGREEMENTS OVER PLAYER RECRUITMENT WITH WHICH DIRECTOR OF FOOTBALL, A FORMER *ENGLAND* INTERNATIONAL?

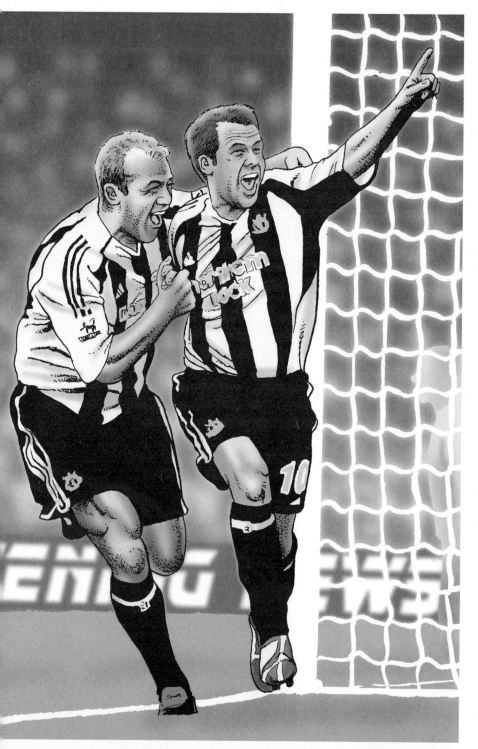

BAD BOYS, BAD BOYS

CRAIG BELLAMY WAS A MAGNET FOR MAYHEM, FREQUENTLY AT LOGGERHEADS WITH THE HIERARCHY AT HIS NUMEROUS CLUBS. HE ONCE THREW A CHAIR AT *NEWCASTLE* COACH *JOHN CARVER*, WAS LATER SENT PACKING BY MANAGER *GRAEME SOUNESS*, WALKED OUT ON *WEST HAM'S GIANFRANCO ZOLA* AND WAS BANISHED BY *MANCHESTER CITY'S ROBERTO MANCINI*. THE MOST INFAMOUS INCIDENT IN *BELLAMY'S* LITANY OF MISDEEDS CAME WHEN HE DRUNKENLY ATTACKED *LIVERPOOL* TEAMMATE *JOHN ARNE RIISE* WITH A GOLF CLUB, EARNING HIMSELF THE NICKNAME *"THE NUTTER WITH THE PUTTER"*.

1 WHICH *NEWCASTLE* MANAGER WAS FINED £100,000 BY THE CLUB AND PICKED UP A SEVEN-GAME BAN AND A FURTHER £60,000 FINE FROM *THE FA* FOR HEADBUTTING *HULL CITY'S DAVID MEYLER*?

2 WHICH HARDMAN STRIKER, WHO HAD NUMEROUS BRUSHES WITH THE LAW FOR ON AND OFF-FIELD INCIDENTS, HOSPITALISED BURGLARS IN TWO SEPARATE INCIDENTS AT HIS HOME IN THE EARLY 2000S?

3 WHICH STRIKER WAS ALLEGEDLY INVOLVED IN AN ALTERCATION DURING TRAINING IN 2010 THAT LEFT HIM WITH A BROKEN HAND AND TEAMMATE *STEVEN TAYLOR* WITH A BROKEN JAW?

4 WHOSE NUMEROUS BRUSHES WITH AUTHORITY HAVE INCLUDED RECEIVING A SIX-MONTH JAIL SENTENCE FOLLOWING A VIOLENT ALTERCATION IN LIVERPOOL IN LATE 2007?

5 WHICH STRIKER'S TROUBLED PRIVATE LIFE HAS SPANNED BEING INCARCERATED FOR INVOLVEMENT IN ARMED ROBBERY AS A TEENAGER, THROUGH NUMEROUS BRUSHES WITH THE LAW, TO SERVING A PRISON SENTENCE FOR FRAUD IN 2017?

6 NAME THE HARDMAN BRICKLAYER-TURNED-STRIKER, SIGNED TO *NEWCASTLE* AS A REPLACEMENT FOR *CHRIS WADDLE*, WHO SUPPLEMENTED HIS INCOME BY PARTICIPATING IN BARE-KNUCKLE BOXING BOUTS, WHO BOTH *VINNIE JONES* AND *NEIL RUDDOCK* SAY WAS THEIR MOST TERRIFYING OPPONENT.

7 FOLLOWING A BRAWL IN A NEWCASTLE NIGHTCLUB IN 2018, WHICH WINGER WAS GIVEN A 10-MONTH JAIL TERM, SUSPENDED FOR 12 MONTHS, AND ORDERED TO CARRY OUT 100 HOURS OF UNPAID WORK AND TO PAY £800 COSTS?

8 WHICH TWO *LEEDS* PLAYERS, BOTH OF WHOM WENT ON TO PLAY FOR *NEWCASTLE*, WENT ON TRIAL TWICE IN 2001 AFTER AN ASIAN STUDENT WAS SEVERELY INJURED, ONE BEING ACQUITTED AND THE OTHER CONVICTED OF AFFRAY?

TOONERS & GOONERS

WHEN **ARSENAL** SIGNED THE PROLIFIC **MALCOLM MACDONALD** FROM **NEWCASTLE** IN 1976, THE AGREED FEE WAS *"ONE THIRD OF A MILLION POUNDS"*, A CHEQUE IN THE AMOUNT OF £333,333.33 WAS DULY PREPARED FOR THE **ARSENAL** CHAIRMAN TO SIGN ... BUT HE INSISTED THAT THE AMOUNT BE AMENDED TO £333,333.34 TO AVOID ANY POSSIBILITY OF THE DEAL BEING DERAILED OVER A MINOR QUIBBLE! HAVING WON THE GOLDEN BOOT WITH *"THE MAGPIES"*, **MACDONALD** REPEATED THE FEAT IN HIS FIRST SEASON AT **HIGHBURY**.

IDENTIFY THESE OTHERS WHO PLAYED FOR **ARSENAL** AND **NEWCASTLE**:

1 LEFT-BACK CAPPED 86 TIMES BY **ENGLAND**.

2 HIS 1960 TRANSFER TO **ARSENAL** FROM **NEWCASTLE** BECAME A LANDMARK LEGAL CASE IN PLAYERS' RIGHTS.

3 CENTRE-BACK CAPPED 73 TIMES BY **ENGLAND**, HE BEGAN HIS PLAYING DAYS AT **SPURS** AND ENDED THEM WITH **NEWCASTLE**.

4 **ARSENAL** YOUNGSTER WHO WENT ON TO WIN THE PREMIER LEAGUE GOLDEN BOOT WITH **NEWCASTLE** IN 1994.

5 FOLLOWING A SUCCESSFUL LOAN SPELL, A £25 MILLION SIGNING TO **NEWCASTLE** FROM **ARSENAL** IN 2021.

6 SIGNED TO **NEWCASTLE** FROM **LILLE** IN EARLY 2013, **FRANCE** INTERNATIONAL RIGHT-BACK WHO JOINED **ARSENAL** IN 2014.

7 CENTRAL DEFENDER, SIGNED FROM **BARNSLEY**, WHO REACHED FA CUP AND LEAGUE CUP FINALS WITH **NEWCASTLE** BEFORE JOINING **ARSENAL** IN 1976.

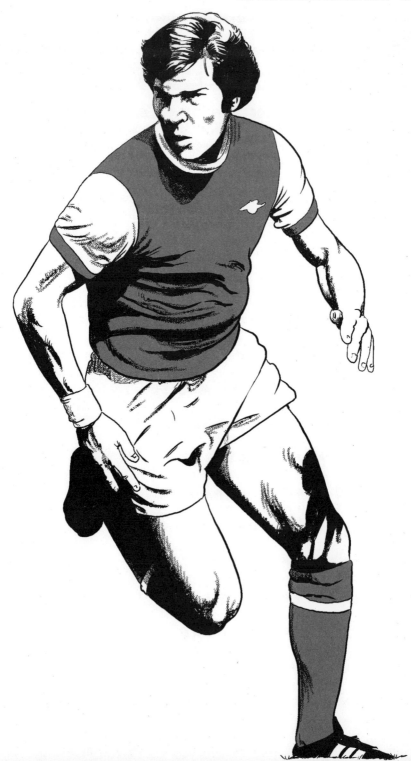

TO VICTOR GO THE SPOILS

WITH HIS SUCCESS IN THE 2006 INTERTOTO CUP, **GLENN ROEDER** BECAME THE FIRST MANAGER TO WIN A TROPHY FOR **NEWCASTLE** SINCE 1969. IT WASN'T ENOUGH TO SECURE HIS JOB -- WITHIN FIVE MONTHS HE HAD BEEN SUCCEEDED BY **SAM ALLARDYCE**.

GLENN'S MIDDLE NAME WAS **VICTOR**. DO YOU KNOW THE MIDDLE NAMES OF THE FOLLOWING?

1   OBAFEMI * * * * * * * * * MARTINS

2   TITUS * * * * * * * BRAMBLE

3   KIERON * * * * * * * * DYER

4   KENNETH * * * * * * * * * DALGLISH

5   CHRISTOPHER * * * * * * WADDLE

6   PETER * * * * * * BEARDSLEY

7   JAMAL * * * * * * LEWIS

8   ALLAN * * * * * * SAINT-MAXIMIN

9   ALAN * * * * * * GOWLING

10   JOHN * * * * * * * HENDRIE

11   NOLBERTO * * * * * * SOLANO

12   MALCOLM * * * MACDONALD

13   CRAIG * * * * * * * BELLAMY

14   YOAN * * * * * * * GOUFFRAN

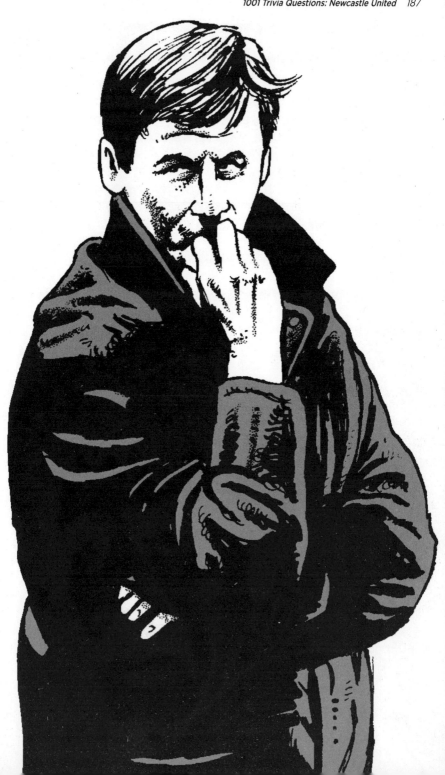

MANY HAPPY RETURNS!

HAVING LAUNCHED HIS CAREER AT *BURY*, *TERRY MCDERMOTT* JOINED *NEWCASTLE* IN 1973. HAVING PLAYED AGAINST *LIVERPOOL* IN THE 1974 FA CUP FINAL, HE JOINED THE MERSEYSIDERS LATER THAT SAME YEAR. HE WENT ON TO WIN THREE EUROPEAN CUPS, FIVE LEAGUE TITLES, THE UEFA CUP AND MUCH MORE DURING HIS EIGHT YEARS AT *ANFIELD*, BEFORE RETURNING TO *NEWCASTLE* IN 1982 AND HELPING THE CLUB RETURN TO THE TOP FLIGHT. HE LATER SERVED AS A COACH AT *NEWCASTLE* UNDER A NUMBER OF MANAGERS, INCLUDING *KEVIN KEEGAN* (TWICE), *GRAEME SOUNESS*, *GLENN ROEDER* AND *SAM ALLARDYCE*.

NAME THESE OTHERS WHO HAD TWO SPELLS AS A *NEWCASTLE* PLAYER:

1   1983-87, EITHER SIDE OF SPELLS WITH *LIVERPOOL* AND *EVERTON*, THEN 1993-97

2   1990-98, EITHER SIDE OF SPELLS WITH *BANIK OSTRAVA, SHEFFIELD WEDNESDAY, BRESCIA, COSENZA, PORTSMOUTH, WEST HAM UNITED* AND *BEIRA-MAR*, THEN 2006-07

3   1998-2004, EITHER SIDE OF A SPELL WITH *ASTON VILLA*, THEN 2005-07

4   1977-79, EITHER SIDE OF SPELLS WITH *ABERDEEN, HAMBURGER SV* AND *CELTIC*, THEN 1989-91

5   1990-97, EITHER SIDE OF A SPELL WITH *BOLTON WANDERERS*, THEN 2001-06

6   1971-75 EITHER SIDE OF A SPELL WITH *BIRMINGHAM CITY*, THEN 1978-81

7   2006-11, EITHER SIDE OF SPELLS WITH *LIVERPOOL* AND *WEST HAM UNITED*, THEN 2019-20

8   1964-71, EITHER SIDE OF A SPELL WITH *MIDDLESBROUGH*, THEN 1982-83

9   1981-82 ON LOAN FROM *WEST BROMWICH ALBION*, THEN 1983-84 AFTER SIGNING FROM *SHEFFIELD WEDNESDAY*

10   1988-93, EITHER SIDE OF SPELLS WITH *NOTTINGHAM FOREST, READING, MANCHESTER CITY* AND *WREXHAM*, THEN 1999-2000

11   1990-97, EITHER SIDE OF SPELLS WITH *SUNDERLAND* AND *FULHAM*, THEN 2005-06

PLAYER OF THE YEAR

HAVING EARNED A DEGREE IN ECONOMICS FROM MANCHESTER UNIVERSITY WHILE PLAYING FOR **MANCHESTER UNITED**, **ALAN GOWLING'S** NICKNAME IN THE DRESSING ROOM WAS **"BAMBER"** AFTER **BAMBER GASCOIGNE**, THE HOST OF TV'S **"UNIVERSITY CHALLENGE"**.

IN 1976, **GOWLING** WAS THE INAUGURAL **NEWCASTLE UNITED PLAYER OF THE YEAR**, AS VOTED FOR BY MEMBERS OF THE OFFICIAL SUPPORTERS' CLUB. OVER THE YEARS, **ALAN SHEARER** WON THE AWARD THREE TIMES, AND **KEVIN KEEGAN**, **PETER BEARDSLEY** AND **SHAY GIVEN** TWICE. IDENTIFY THESE WINNERS BY YEAR AND NATIONALITY:

1 2002: PERUVIAN MIDFIELDER

2 2004: FRENCH DEFENDER

3 2008: FRENCH DEFENDER CAPPED BY **SENEGAL**

4 2009: FRENCH DEFENDER CAPPED BY **CAMEROON**

5 2010: SPANISH LEFT-BACK

6 2011: ARGENTINE CENTRE-BACK

7 2012: DUTCH GOALKEEPER

8 2013: ITALIAN LEFT-BACK

9 2015: DUTCH RIGHT-BACK

10 2019: VENEZUELAN STRIKER

11 2020: SLOVAK GOALKEEPER

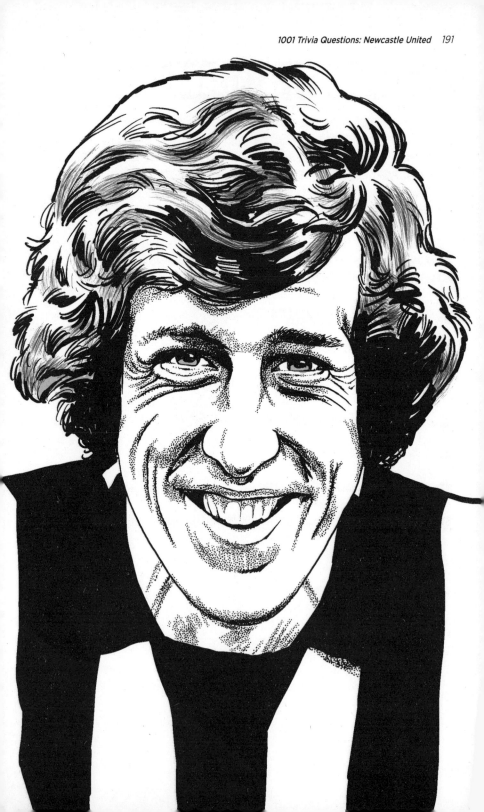

GULLIT'S GAMBLES

FOLLOWING THE DISMISSAL OF **KENNY DALGLISH** IN 1998,
NEWCASTLE TURNED TO **RUUD GULLIT**, THE 36-YEAR-OLD GLOBAL
SUPERSTAR WHO HAD WON THE FA CUP WITH **CHELSEA** IN HIS FIRST FORAY
INTO MANAGEMENT. APPARENTLY DETERMINED TO STAMP HIS AUTHORITY
ON THE CLUB, **GULLIT** SIDELINED VETERANS **STUART PEARCE**
AND **JOHN BARNES** AND SENT **ROB LEE** TO TRAIN WITH THE KIDS.
WHEN HE DROPPED STRIKERS **ALAN SHEARER** AND **DUNCAN
FERGUSON** FOR THE TYNE-WEAR DERBY -- AND HIS SELECTION LOST TO
SUNDERLAND -- THE WRITING WAS ON THE WALL AND HE RESIGNED
A FEW DAYS LATER, ONE YEAR AND A DAY AFTER BEING APPOINTED.

IDENTIFY THESE **RUUD GULLIT** SIGNINGS:

1   NOVEMBER, 1998: £8 MILLION FROM **EVERTON**

2   JULY, 1999: £6 MILLION FROM **IPSWICH TOWN**

3   JUNE, 1999: £4.7 MILLION FROM **PARIS SAINT-GERMAIN**

4   JUNE, 1999: £6.7 MILLION FROM **RCD MALLORCA**

5   FEBRUARY, 1999: £3.5 MILLION FROM **CROATIA ZAGREB**

6   JANUARY, 1999: £4 MILLION FROM **PARIS SAINT-GERMAIN**

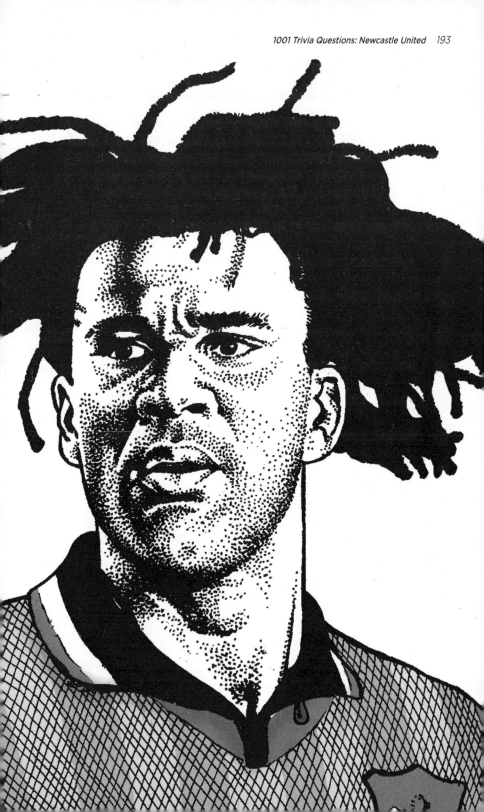

BIG SAM'S SHOPPING

AUSTRALIA STRIKER **MARK VIDUKA**, WHO HAD WON HONOURS WITH **DINAMO ZAGREB** AND **CELTIC** AND BANGED IN GOALS FOR **LEEDS UNITED** AND **MIDDLESBROUGH**, WAS **SAM ALLARDYCE'S** FIRST SIGNING WHEN APPOINTED **NEWCASTLE** BOSS IN 2007. **VIDUKA'S** TWO INJURY-RAVAGED YEARS AT THE CLUB ENDED WITH RELEGATION.

IDENTIFY THESE OTHER **SAM ALLARDYCE** SIGNINGS:

1 AUGUST, 2007: £6 MILLION FROM **MANCHESTER UNITED**

2 AUGUST, 2007: £6.3 MILLION FROM **VILLARREAL**

3 JUNE, 2007: £5.8 MILLION FROM **MANCHESTER CITY**

4 JUNE, 2007: £2.9 MILLION FROM **PARIS SAINT-GERMAIN**

5 AUGUST, 2007: £2 MILLION FROM **MARSEILLE**

6 AUGUST, 2007: £2 MILLION FROM **BOLTON WANDERERS**

7 JANUARY, 2008: £1.22 MILLION FROM **ZALAEGERSZEG**

8 JANUARY, 2008: £270,000 FROM **SWINDON TOWN**

9 JULY, 2007: FREE TRANSFER FROM **CHELSEA**

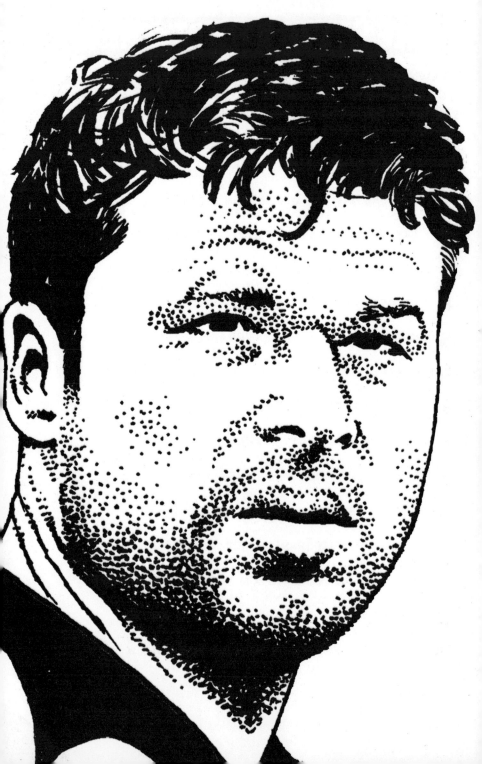

KENNY'S CAPTURES

SHAY GIVEN WAS ONE OF THE FIRST SIGNINGS BY *KENNY DALGLISH* FOLLOWING HIS 1997 APPOINTMENT AS *NEWCASTLE* MANAGER. THREE YEARS EARLIER, DURING HIS TENURE AS *BLACKBURN ROVERS* BOSS, *DALGLISH* HAD SIGNED *GIVEN* FROM *CELTIC*.

IDENTIFY THESE OTHER *DALGLISH* SIGNINGS TO *NEWCASTLE*:

1 FEBRUARY, 1998: £5.5 MILLION FROM *EVERTON*

2 JULY, 1997: £4.5 MILLION FROM *INTERNAZIONALE*

3 JANUARY, 1998: £3.71 MILLION FROM *AC MILAN*

4 JULY, 1997: £3.51 MILLION FROM *HEERENVEEN*

5 MARCH, 1997: £2 MILLION FROM *BRADFORD CITY*

6 JANUARY, 1998: £1.5 MILLION FROM *STOKE CITY*

7 MARCH, 1998: £2 MILLION FROM *OLYMPIACOS*

8 JUNE, 1998: £420,000 FROM *PANATHINAIKOS*

9 JUNE, 1997: £360,000 FROM *FEYENOORD*

10 JULY, 1997: FREE TRANSFER FROM *AEK ATHENS*

11 AUGUST, 1997: FREE TRANSFER FROM *LIVERPOOL*

12 JULY, 1997: FREE TRANSFER FROM *NOTTINGHAM FOREST*

13 AUGUST, 1997: FREE TRANSFER FROM *LEEDS UNITED*

14 AUGUST, 1998: £5.5 MILLION FROM *BAYERN MUNICH*

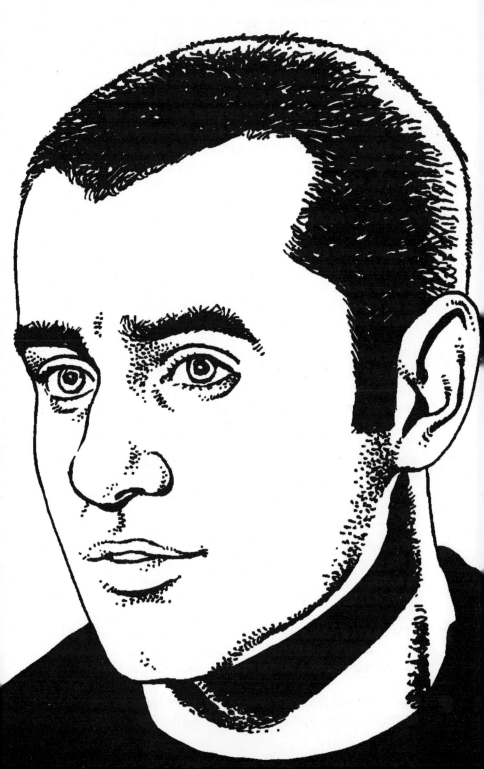

GOING DUTCH

BROTHERS **SIEM** AND **LUUK DE JONG** WERE BORN IN AIGLE, SWITZERLAND TO DUTCH PARENTS WHO PLAYED PROFESSIONAL VOLLEYBALL AND MOVED BACK TO THE NETHERLANDS WHEN THE BOYS WERE YOUNG. THE BROTHERS HAVE BOTH REPRESENTED THE **NETHERLANDS** AT INTERNATIONAL LEVEL, HAVE PLAYED WITH AND AGAINST EACH OTHER AT CLUB LEVEL ... AND WERE BOTH ON THE BOOKS AT NEWCASTLE, ALTHOUGH NEITHER PLAYER'S STAY WAS PRODUCTIVE.

IDENTIFY THESE **NEWCASTLE** PLAYERS WITH DUTCH CONNECTIONS:

1 LEFT-BACK WHO BECAME THE YOUNGEST PLAYER TO THAT POINT TO APPEAR IN THE EUROPEAN CHAMPIONSHIP WHEN HE TURNED OUT FOR THE **NETHERLANDS** AT EURO 2012, HIS SEASON-LONG LOAN TO **NEWCASTLE** FROM **EINTRACHT FRANKFURT** IN THE 2019-20 SEASON WAS CURTAILED BY A SERIOUS ACL INJURY.

2 DUTCH INTERNATIONAL LEFT-BACK WHO WAS LOANED OUT BY **CHELSEA** TO **NEWCASTLE** AND A NUMBER OF OTHER CLUBS BEFORE JOINING **SUNDERLAND** IN 2014. HE WAS SOLD TO **CRYSTAL PALACE** IN A £9 MILLION DEAL IN 2017 AND MOVED ON TO **GALATASARAY** IN THE SUMMER OF 2021.

3 GOALKEEPER WHO BEGAN HIS CAREER AT **NAC BREDA** AND LATER MANAGED THE CLUB AFTER HIS PLAYING DAYS WERE OVER, HE SPENT FOUR YEARS AT **NEWCASTLE**, INVARIABLY BEHIND **SHAY GIVEN** AND **STEVE HARPER** IN THE PECKING ORDER.

4 CAPPED 34 TIMES BY THE **NETHERLANDS**, FOR WHOM HE PLAYED IN THE 2014 WORLD CUP, AFTER WHICH HE JOINED **"THE MAGPIES"**. HE MOVED ON TO **WATFORD** TWO YEARS LATER, FOLLOWING **NEWCASTLE'S** RELEGATION.

5 **NEWCASTLE** GOALKEEPER WHO WAS FAMOUSLY BROUGHT ON AS A 120TH-MINUTE SUBSTITUTE IN A 2014 WORLD CUP QUARTER-FINAL AND HELPED SECURE A DUTCH PENALTY SHOOTOUT VICTORY.

6 EURO 2000 GOLDEN BOOT WINNER CAPPED 79 TIMES BY THE **NETHERLANDS**, HE JOINED **NEWCASTLE** IN 2004.

7 2015 DUTCH FOOTBALLER OF THE YEAR, AFTER WHICH HE SPENT A SEASON AT **NEWCASTLE**, HE JOINED **PARIS SAINT-GERMAIN** IN 2021 AFTER WINNING THE CHAMPIONS LEAGUE, THE PREMIER LEAGUE AND MORE WITH **LIVERPOOL**.

THE EVER-PRESENTS

BELFAST-BORN **BILL MCCRACKEN**, A POWERFUL DEFENDER WHO CAPTAINED **NEWCASTLE** AND **IRELAND** AND IS CREDITED WITH INVENTING THE OFFSIDE TRAP, WON THREE LEAGUE TITLES AND THE FA CUP DURING HIS TWO DECADES WITH **"THE MAGPIES"**. HE WENT ON TO MANAGE **HULL CITY**, **GATESHEAD**, **MILLWALL** AND ALDERSHOT BEFORE RETURNING TO **NEWCASTLE** AS A SCOUT.

MCCRACKEN'S 432 GAMES FOR **NEWCASTLE** BETWEEN 1904 AND 1924 PLACE HIM FIFTH ON THE CLUB'S ALL-TIME APPEARANCE LIST. IDENTIFY THE FOUR PLAYERS WHO MADE MORE APPEARANCES THAN **MCCRACKEN** FOR **NEWCASTLE**:

1 496 GAMES (1904-1922): SCOTTISH GOALKEEPER WHO WON THREE LEAGUE TITLES AND THE FA CUP. HE LATER MANAGED **PRESTON NORTH END** AND **KARLSRUHER FV**, WINNING NUMEROUS HONOURS WITH THE LATTER.

2 472 GAMES (1910-1929): IN 1925, AGED 35, THE LEFT-BACK BECAME THE OLDEST PLAYER TO MAKE HIS **ENGLAND** DEBUT, A RECORD HE HELD UNTIL 1950.

3 462 GAMES (1997-2009): **REPUBLIC OF IRELAND** GOALKEEPER.

4 457 GAMES (1962-1975): WENT ON TO WIN THE EUROPEAN CUP AND LEAGUE TITLE WITH **NOTTINGHAM FOREST** AND MANAGE **LEYTON ORIENT**, **NOTTINGHAM FOREST** AND **MANCHESTER CITY**.

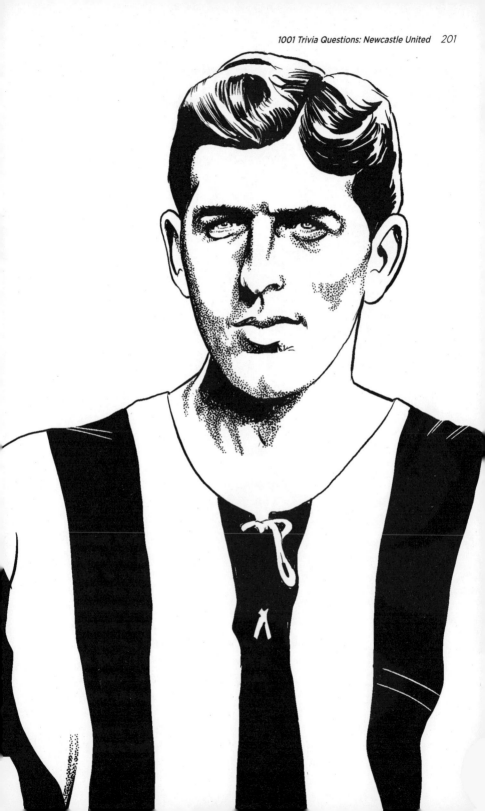

CELEB SUPPORTERS

ROCK SUPERSTAR **STING** MAY HAVE LEFT TYNESIDE IN THE LATE 1970S TO SEEK GLOBAL FAME AND FORTUNE BUT HE REMAINS A PASSIONATE **NEWCASTLE UNITED** SUPPORTER. THE FORMER FRONTMAN WITH **THE POLICE** HAS STATED THAT HIS ALL-TIME HERO IS **BOBBY MONCUR.**

IDENTIFY THESE OTHER CELEBRITY **NEWCASTLE** FANS:

1 FORMER *GIRLS ALOUD* MEMBER WHO WAS AT ONE TIME MARRIED TO A *CHELSEA* AND *ENGLAND* DEFENDER.

2 ACTOR WHOSE ROLES RANGE FROM *PC "FANCY" SMITH* ON TV'S *"Z CARS"* AND *PRINCE VULTAN* IN *"FLASH GORDON"*, TO VOICING *GRAMPY RABBIT* IN *"PEPPA PIG"*.

3 DAUGHTER OF A FORMER MANAGER OF THE *WALES* TEAM, SHE BECAME ONE OF TV'S MOST SUCCESSFUL SPORTS PRESENTERS.

4 *MCPARTLIN* AND *DONNELLY*.

5 REPLACED *BON SCOTT* IN *AC/DC*.

6 *JAMES MICHAEL ALOYSIUS BRADFORD*, AKA *LEONARD JEFFREY "OZ" OSBORNE* AND *JED SHEPHERD*.

7 SON OF A COUNTY DURHAM FARM LABOURER WHO ALSO LOOKED AFTER PIT PONIES, MUSIC SUPERSTAR WHO RAISED HIS FOUR SONS -- *OTIS, ISAAC, TARA* AND *MERLIN* -- TO BE STAUNCH *NEWCASTLE UNITED* SUPPORTERS.

8 AKA *FUSILIER DAVE TUCKER, D.I. DAVE CREEGAN, DR. TONY HILL, COLIN ARMSTRONG* AND *GEORDIE KEATING*.

9 ARTIST WHO HIT BIG WITH *"HOLD BACK THE RIVER"* IN 2014.

10 FLAMBOYANT HORSE RACING PUNDIT AND TV PERSONALITY.

1001 ANSWERS

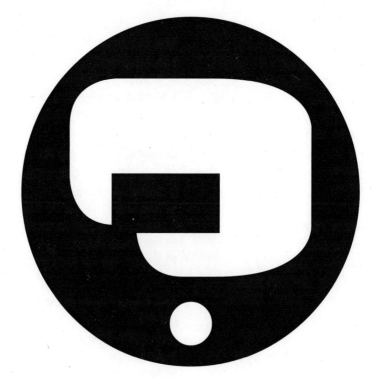

The Gallowgate Giant (pg 2)

1. Chris Nicholl   2. Jimmy Greaves
3. Ian Branfoot   4. Chris Sutton
5. "Creosoting the fence"
6. Ray Harford   7. Aston Villa,
Charlton Athletic   8. Celtic
9. Thierry Henry, Eric Cantona,
Roy Keane, Frank Lampard,
Dennis Bergkamp, Steven Gerrard,
David Beckham

King Kev (pg 4)

1. Scunthorpe United
2. Bill Shankly   3. Everton
4. Billy Bremner   5. Kenny Dalglish
6. Hamburger SV
7. Lawrie McMenemy
8. Arthur Cox
9. Liverpool
10. Australia

Howay The Young Lads! (pg 6)

1. Bobby Moncur
2. Joe Allon   3. Gary Kelly
4. David Craig   5. Kevin Scott
6. Dave Turner   7. Brian Tinnion
8. Alan Suddick

They Crossed The Tyne-Wear Divide (pg 8)

1. Jack Colback   2. Lee Clark
3. Paul Bracewell   4. Louis Saha
5. Barry Venison   6. Len Shackleton
7. Chris Waddle

The Money Makers! (pg 10)

1. Moussa Sissoko
2. Mathieu Debuchy
3. Dietmar Hamann
4. Ayoze Pérez   5. Shay Given
6. Georginio Wijnaldum
7. Duncan Ferguson   8. Andy Cole
9. Yohan Cabaye
10. Jonathan Woodgate
11. Aleksandar Mitrović
12. Demba Ba   13. James Milner
14. Kieron Dyer
15. Andros Townsend
16. David Batty

One To Watch! (pg 12)

1. Montpellier   2. Lille   3. Bordeaux
4. Monaco   5. Marseille   6. Nancy
7. Montpellier   8. Reims   9. Toulouse
10. Lille   11. Rennes   12. Bordeaux

Colombia's Finest (pg 14)

1. Liverpool (2)   2. Galatasaray
3. Sevilla   4. Liverpool
5. Tottenham Hotspur   6. Feyenoord
7. Liverpool   8. Tottenham Hotspur
9. Tottenham Hotspur
10. Bayern Munich and Liverpool

PFA Young Player of the Year (pg 16)

1. Ian Rush   2. Paul Gascoigne
3. Andy Cole   4. Michael Owen
5. Jermaine Jenas   6. Scott Parker
7. James Milner

Sheffield Steal (pg 18)

1. Pat Heard   2. Imre Varadi
3. Gary Megson   4. Achraf Lazaar
5. Tommy Craig   6. Rolando Aarons
7. David Mills   8. Ronnie Starling
9. Jacob Murphy   10. Jackie Sinclair

Greece Is The Word (pg 20)

1. Islam Slimani
2. Keith Gillespie
3. Steve Howey
4. Ayoze Pérez 5. Ken Leek
6. Norbert Solano
7. Les Ferdinand
8. Paul Kitson
9. Danny Simpson

A Gallic Great (pg 22)

1. Alan Shearer
2. Les Ferdinand
3. Faustino Asprilla
4. David Batty 5. Darren Peacock
6. Warren Barton 7. Paul Kitson
8. Andy Cole 9. Ruel Fox
10. Shaka Hislop 11. Peter Beardsley
12. Rob Lee 13. Fabricio Coloccini
14. Jonás Gutiérrez
15. Danny Guthrie
16. Sébastien Bassong

Howe-Way The Lads! (pg 24)

1. Osvaldo Ardiles 2. Alan Pardew
3. Joe Kinnear 4. Willie McFaul
5. Glenn Roeder 6. Bobby Robson
7. Joe Harvey 8. Steve Bruce
9. Jack Charlton 10. Arthur Cox

England Expects (pg 26)

1. Michael Owen
2. Kenny Sansom
3. John Barnes 4. Stuart Pearce
5. Sol Campbell 6. Alan Shearer
7. Chris Waddle 8. James Milner
9. Peter Beardsley
10. Paul Gascoigne

Hey, Big Spender! (pg 28)

1. Bournemouth
2. Atlanta United
3. Nice 4. Internazionale
5. Blackburn Rovers 6. PSV
7. Norwich City 8. Anderlecht
9. Marseille 10. Arsenal
11. Crystal Palace
12. Real Madrid
13. Bournemouth
14. Tottenham Hotspur
15. Swansea City
16. Norwich City

All-Time Highs (pg 30)

1. Len White
2. Hughie Gallacher
3. Malcolm Macdonald
4. Peter Beardsley
5. Bobby Mitchell
6. Tom McDonald 7. Neil Harris
8. Bryan Robson

Paying Their Dues (pg 32)

1. Alan Shearer 2. Alan Pardew
3. Ruud Gullit 4. Joe Harvey
5. Steve Clarke 6. Graeme Souness
7. Rafael Benítez 8. Bobby Robson
9. Colin Suggett 10. Willie McFaul

Hall of Famers (pg 34)

1. Paul Gascoigne 2. Kevin Keegan
3. Alan Shearer 4. John Barnes
5. Ian Rush 6. Peter Beardsley
7. Len Shackleton
8. Hughie Gallacher
9. Michael Owen 10. Ivor Allchurch
11. Stuart Pearce 12. Gary Speed

Villains! (pg 36)

1. Shay Given
2. Charles N'Zogbia
3. Aaron Hughes
4. David Ginola
5. Wayne Routledge
6. Marlon Harewood
7. Stephen Ireland   8. Franz Carr
9. Habib Beye   10. Ciaran Clark
11. Ronny Johnsen   12. Peter Withe

Blue and White Hoops, Black and White Stripes (pg 38)

1. Darren Peacock
2. Joey Barton   3. Kenny Sansom
4. Ian Stewart   5. Loïc Rémy
6. Wayne Routledge
7. Fitz Hall

Nobby from Lima (pg 40)

1. Brazil   2. Chile
3. United States   4. Paraguay
5. Uruguay   6. Venezuela
7. Martinique   8. Trinidad and Tobago   9. Guyana   10. Canada
11. Chile   12. Brazil   13. Colombia
14. Montserrat   15. United States

Cottagers (pg 42)

1. Philippe Albert
2. Aleksandar Mitrović
3. Alain Goma
4. Damien Duff
5. Gary Brazil

Geordie Red Men (pg 44)

1. Georginio Wijnaldum
2. John Barnes   3. José Enrique
4. Danny Guthrie

Band of Merry Men (pg 46)

1. Michael Chopra
2. Frank Clark   3. Gary Megson
4. Jermaine Jenas   5. James Perch
6. Jack Colback

Paperback Writers (pg 48)

1. Keith Gillespie
2. Joey Barton   3. Kieron Dyer
4. Shay Glven   5. Terry McDermott
6. Gavin Peacock   7. Len Shackleton
8. Andrew Cole
9. Graeme Souness
10. Bobby Robson
11. Michael Owen   12. Les Ferdinand
13. Kenny Sansom

The Boys of '99 (pg 50)

1. Hull City   2. Portsmouth
3. Leicester City   4. Manchester City
5. Paris Saint-Germain
6. Derby County
7. Bolton Wanderers   8. Aston Villa
9. Wolverhampton Wanderers
10. Manchester City
11. Derby County   12. Porto
13. Watford   14. Everton

Black & White Cherries (pg 52)

1. Gavin Peacock   2. Matt Ritchie
3. Dan Gosling   4. Ryan Fraser
5. Charlie Woods   6. Dick Keith

Kenny D (pg 54)

1. Jim Smith   2. Kevin Keegan
3. Ruud Gullit   4. Graeme Souness
5. Chris Hughton   6. Sam Allardyce
7. Steve McClaren   8. Rafael Benítez
9. Eddie Howe

Champions of Europe (pg 56)

1. Internazionale 2010
2. Liverpool 2019
3. Manchester United 2008
4. Liverpool 1977, 1981, 1987
5. AC Milan 2003
6. Manchester United 1999
7. Nottingham Forest 1979
8. Liverpool 1977
9. Liverpool 2005
10. Manchester United 1999
11. Manchester United 1999
12. Real Madrid 2000, 2002
13. Liverpool 2019
14. Aston Villa 1982

Bruce Buys (pg 58)

1. TSG Hoffenheim
2. Nice   3. Tottenham Hotspur
4. FC Schalke 04   5. West Ham
6. Amiens   7. Eintracht Frankfurt
8. Norwich City   9. Motherwell
10. Burnley   11. Bolton Wanderers
12. Internazionale

The Wizard of Nod (pg 60)

1. Wyn Davies
2. Len Sghackleton
3. Fitz Hall   4. David Kelly
5. Paul Goddard
6. Peter Beardsley
7. Scott Sellars   8. Bobby Mitchell
9. Mick Martin   10. Stuart Pearce
11. Oguchi Onyewu
12. Jonás Gutiérrez
13. Alan Gowling
14. Ron McGarry

Toffeemen (pg 62)

1. Duncan Ferguson
2. George Heslop
3. Alessandro Pistone
4. Sylvain Distin
5. Dan Gosling
6. Steve Watson
7. Paul Bracewell
8. Kevin Sheedy
9. Imre Varadi

Goalgetter Greats (pg 64)

1. Jackie Milburn
2. Len White
3. Hughie Gallacher
4. Malcolm Macdonald
5. Peter Beardsley
6. Tommy McDonald
7. Bobby Mitchell
8. Neil Harris
9. Pop Robson

The Spain Drain (pg 66)

1. Mikel Merino
2. Jonathan Woodgate
3. Jonás Gutiérrez
4. Patrick Kluivert
5. Emmanuel Rivière
6. José Enrique
7. Nacho González
8. Kieran Trippier

Extracurricular Activities (pg 68)

1. Nolberto Solano
2. Fitz Hall   3. "Hero To Zero"
4. Lindisfarne
5. "Diamond Lights"
6. Basile Boli
7. "Boys From The Blackstuff"

Rafa's Men (pg 70)

1. Liverpool 2. Chelsea
3. Real Madrid 4. Valencia
5. Internazionale 6. Napoli
7. Everton 8. Newcastle
9. Dalian Professional 10. Chelsea
11. Chelsea 12. Internazionale
13. Newcastle 14. Napoli

Red Devil Magpies (pg 72)

1. Louis Saha 2. Keith Gillespie
3. Giuseppe Rossi 4. Albert Scanlon
5. Andy Cole 6. Gabriel Obertan
7. Alan Smith 8. Liam O'Brien

The Chinese Connection (pg 74)

1. Demba Ba 2. Paul Gascoigne
3. Cheick Tioté 4. Salomón Rondón
5. Papiss Cissé 6. Rafael Benítez

Jonjo Joins (pg 76)

1. Nottingham Forest 2. Gent
3. Aston Villa 4. Blackburn Rovers
5. Nottingham Forest
6. Anderlecht 7. Tottenham Hotspur
8. Sunderland 9. Ajax
10. Bournemouth 11. Arsenal
12. Hull City 13. Bordeaux
14. Chelsea 15. Crystal Palace
16. Tenerife 17. Ipswich Town
18. Anderlecht

Bald Eagle Buys (pg 78)

1. Celtic 2. Portsmouth
3. Baník Ostrava 4. QPR
5. Preston North End
6. Bournemouth 7. Aberdeen
8. Celtic 9. Southampton
10. Aarhus GF

Making an Entrance (pg 80)

1. Micky Quinn 2. Duncan Ferguson
3. Georginio Wijnaldum
4. Kevin Keegan 5. Les Ferdinand
6. Matty Longstaff
7. Papiss Demba Cissé
8. Malcolm Macdonald

Mundial Magpies 1 (pg 82)

1. England 2. Chile 3. England
4. England 5. England
6. Northern Ireland 7. England
8. Northern Ireland 9. Wales
10. Northern Ireland 11. Wales
12. England 13. England

Mundial Magpies 2 (pg 84)

1. Scotland 2. Scotland
3. Argentina 4. Scotland
5. Northern Ireland 6. England
7. England 8. Northern Ireland
9. England 10. Scotland
11. England 12. England
13. Northern Ireland 14. Belgium
15. England 16. Republic of Ireland
17. Netherlands
18. Republic of Ireland
19. England 20. Republic of Ireland

Mundial Magpies 3 (pg 86)

1. England 2. Germany 3. Norway
4. England 5. Croatia 6. England
7. Chile 8. England 9. Netherlands
10. England 11. Scotland 12. France
13. Nigeria 14. Colombia
15. Scotland

Mundial Magpies 4 (pg 88)

1. England   2. Cameroon
3. Senegal   4. Spain
5. Republic of Ireland
6. Portugal   7. Sweden
8. Turkey   9. Senegal
10. Denmark   11. England
12. Republic of Ireland
13. Paraguay   14. Denmark
15. Senegal

Mundial Magpies 5 (pg 90)

1. United States   2. England
3. Trinidad and Tobago
4. Australia   5. England   6. France
7. Czech Republic   8. France
9. Australia   10. Ivory Coast
11. Uruguay   12. Nigeria
13. Cameroon   14. Argentina
15. Ivory Coast   16. England

Mundial Magpies 6 (pg 92)

1. Netherlands   2. France
3. Australia   4. United States
5. France   6. Netherlands
7. Ghana   8. France   9. England
10. France   11. Netherlands
12. Nigeria   13. France
14. Serbia   15. France

The Young Ones (pg 94)

1. Carl Cort   2. Stuart Pearce
3. David Rozehnal   4. Shola Ameobi
5. Alan Shearer   6. Paul Goddard
7. Steven Taylor

Hot Seats! (pg 96)

1. Bobby Gould   2. Don Mackay
3. Dick Advocaat   4. Tony Pulis
5. Roy McFarland
6. Joe Royle
7. Carlo Ancelotti
8. Ian Holloway
9. Roberto Di Matteo
10. Harry Redknapp

Souness Spendings (pg 98)

1. Albert Luque   2. Jean-Alain
Boumsong   3. Scott Parker
4. Emre Belözoglu
5. Amdy Fayé   6. Nolberto Solano
7. Celestine Babayaro
8. Craig Moore   9. Lee Clark

Aussie Magpies (pg 100)

1. Melbourne City
2. Melbourne Knights
3. West Adelaide
4. Melbourne Knights
5. Melbourne City
6. Blacktown City
7. South Coast United,
Bulli FC and Balgownie Rangers

Well, I Never ... (pg 102)

1. Gavin Peacock
2. Michael Chopra
3. Philippe Albert
4. Ron McGarry
5. Ruud Gullit
6. Stéphane Guivarc'h
7. Lee Bowyer
8. Faustino "Tino" Asprilla
9. Shaka Hislop

Number 9 (pg 104)

1. Chris Woods
2. Rob Jones
3. Stuart Pearce
4. Martin Keown   5. Des Walker
6. Mark Wright   7. Neil Webb
8. Geoff Thomas   9. Nigel Clough
11. David Hirst
12. Gary Lineker

"You'll Not see Nothing Like The Mighty Wyn..." (pg 106)

1. Robbie Elliott
2. Kevin Nolan
3. Abdoulaye Faye
4. Alan Thompson

Teen Titans (pg 108)

1. Haris Vučkić
2. Robbie Elliott
3. Steve Howey
4. Kazenga LuaLua
5. Paul Gascoigne

World Leaders (pg 110)

1. Ruel Fox   2. Bill McGarry
3. Peter Withe   4. John Barnes
5. Willie McFaul   6. Michael O'Neill
7. Patrick Kluivert   8. Bill McGarry
9. Joe Kinnear   10. Temur Ketsbaia
11. Joe Kinnear   12. Peter Withe

Magpies & Canaries (pg 112)

1. Sébastien Bassong
2. Fraser Forster
3. Paul Dalglish   4. Colin Suggett
5. Grant Hanley   6. Jacob Murphy

"Catch Me If You Can, 'Cause I'm the England Man ..." (pg 114)

1. Guyana   2. Curaçao   3. Burundi
4. DR Congo   5. Martinique
6. Chile   7. Belgium   8. Finland
9. Mali   10. Cyprus
11. Montserrat   12. United States

Country Life (pg 116)

1. Sam Allardyce   2. Kevin Keegan
3. Jack Charlton   4. Bobby Robson
5. Steve McClaren   6. Steve Clarke

It's Hammer Time! (pg 118)

1. Shaka Hislop   2. Nolberto Solano
3. Lee Bowyer   4. Vic Keeble
5. Demba Ba   6. Kieron Dyer

The Goal Merchants (pg 120)

1. Micky Burns   2. Imre Varadi
3. Peter Beardsley   4. Mirandinha
5. Micky Quinn   6. Andy Cole
7. Michael Owen   8. Demba Ba
9. Ayoze Pérez

Imported From Spain (pg 122)

1. Atlético Madrid   2. Mallorca
3. Tenerife   4. Real Madrid
5. Villarreal   6. Mallorca
7. Deportivo de La Coruña
8. Atlético Madrid   9. Barcelona
10. Deportivo de La Coruña

The Bhoys (pg 124)

1. Shay Given   2. John McNamee
3. Mark Viduka   4. Fraser Forster
5. Alan Thompson   6. Craig Bellamy
7. Mark McGhee

The Dragons (pg 126)

1. Gary Speed
2. Craig Bellamy
3. Ivor Allchurch
4. Wyn Davies
5. Paul Bodin
6. Glyn Hodges
7. Malcolm Allen

Back In My Day (pg 128)

1. Graeme Souness
2. Steve Bruce
3. Ruud Gullit
4. Joe Kinnear
5. Sam Allardyce
6. Jack Charlton
7. Kenny Dalglish
8. Chris Hughton
9. Nigel Pearson
10. Kevin Keegan
11. Alan Shearer

Cockerels of the Northeast (pg 130)

1. Andros Townsend
2. Sébastien Bassong
3. Danny Rose
4. Stephen Carr
5. DeAndre Yedlin
6. Ruel Fox
7. Moussa Sissoko

Record Setters (pg 132)

1. Newport County
2. Billy Hampson   3. Andy Cole
4. Alan Pardew
5. Burton Wanderers
6. Jimmy Lawrence
7. Faustino Asprilla
8. Ossie Ardiles

Pavel is a Geordie (pg 134)

1. Slovenia   2. Hungary   3. Iceland
4. Finland   5. Czech Republic
6. Georgia   7. Slovakia   8. Sweden
9. Switzerland

Harvey Ballbanger (pg 136)

1. Middlesbrough
2. Blackpool   3. Linfield
4. Bury   5. Lincoln City
6. Gateshead   7. Portsmouth
8. Huddersfield Town
9. West Ham United
10. Bradford Park Avenue

"Life is So Good in America ..." (pg 138)

1. c   2. a   3. a   4. b   5. b   6. a

City Slickers (pg 140)

1. Joey Barton
2. Laurent Charvet
3. Ray Ranson   4. Antoine Sibierski
5. Wyn Davies   6. Ivor Broadis
7. Steve Howey
8. Tony Cunningham

Bobby's Boys (pg 142)

1. Barcelona   2. Fulham
3. Porto   4. Barcelona   5. PSV
Eindhoven   6. PSV Eindhoven
7. Newcastle United   8. Barcelona
9. Porto   10. Ipswich Town

Magpie Trotters (pg 144)

1. Ron McGarry
2. Abdoulaye Fayé   3. Wyn Davies
4. Sammy Ameobi   5. Scott Sellars

Rafa's Recruits (pg 146)

1. Dwight Gayle
2. Matt Ritchie
3. Jacob Murphy
4. Yoshinori Muto
5. Florian Lejeune
6. Christian Atsu
7. Mikel Merino
8. Federico Fernández
9. Matz Sels   10. Grant Hanley
11. Ciaran Clark
12. DeAndre Yedlin   13. Joselu
14. Mohamed Diamé
15. Javier Manquillo

Wild Rovers (pg 148)

1. Andy Cole
2. Craig Bellamy
3. Zurab Khizanishvili
4. Darren Peacock
5. Kevin Gallacher
6. Danny Simpson

The Job Centre (pg 150)

1. Jim Smith, Bobby Saxton, Kenny Dalglish, Graeme Souness, Sam Allardyce   2. Ruud Gullit, Rafa Benítez   3. Jim Smith, Chris Hughton, Steve Bruce
4. Graeme Souness, Nigel Pearson, Alan Pardew   5. Sam Allardyce, Steve Bruce   6. Chris Hughton, Joe Kinnear, Steve McClaren
7. Ossie Ardiles, Steve Clarke, Sam Allardyce, Alan Pardew
8. Jim Smith, Steve McClaren
9. Kevin Keegan, Bobby Robson
10. Kenny Dalglish, Graeme Souness, Rafa Benítez

Bobby's Buys (pg 152)

1. Laurent Robert
2. Jonathan Woodgate
3. Hugo Viana
4. Carl Cort
5. Jermaine Jenas
6. James Milner
7. Titus Bramble
8. Christian Bassedas
9. Lomana LuaLua
10. Nicky Butt
11. Andrew O'Brien
12. Stephen Carr
13. Clarence Acuña
14. Darren Ambrose
15. Wayne Quinn
16. Charles N'Zogbia
17. Lee Bowyer
18. Patrick Kluivert
19. Ronny Johnsen
20. Michael Bridges

Sur le Continent (pg 154)

1. Juventus   2. Real Madrid
3. Hamburger SV   4. Lazio
5. Hamburger SV
6. Real Madrid
7. Marseille
8. Atlético Madrid

O Brother, Where art Thou? (pg 156)

1. Robledo   2. Guthrie
3. Kennedy   4. Withe
5. Caldwell   6. McClen
7. LuaLua   8. Ameobi
9. Longstaff

Paying Their Dues 2 (pg 158)
1. Joe Kinnear
2. Steve McClaren
3. Osvaldo Ardiles
4. Kevin Keegan   5. Jim Smith
6. Nigel Pearson   7. Sam Allardyce
8. Glenn Roeder   9. Chris Hughton
10. Gordon Lee
11. Terry McDermott
12. Kenny Dalglish
13. Bill McGarry
14. Graeme Jones

Bravehearts (pg 160)
1. Roy Aitken
2. Bobby Moncur
3. Ryan Fraser
4. Grant Hanley
5. Hughie Gallacher
6. Matt Richie
7. Steven Caldwell

Hat-Trick Heroics (pg 162)
1. Peter Beardsley
2. Andy Cole   3. Les Ferdinand
4. Alan Shearer   5. Andy Carroll
6. Kevin Nolan   7. Leon Best
8. Demba Ba
9. Georginio Wijnaldum
10. Ayoze Pérez

Back of the Net! (pg 164)
1. Michael Owen   2. Mick Channon
3. Kevin Keegan   4. John Barnes
5. Jackie Milburn   6. Paul Gascoigne
7. Peter Beardsley   8. Ivor Broadis
9. Malcolm Macdonald
10. Chris Waddle   11. Stuart Pearce
12. Les Ferdinand

Ici C'est Paris (pg 166)
1. Laurent Robert
2. Didier Domi
3. Sylvain Distin
4. Yohan Cabaye
5. David Rozehnal

Cox's Captures (pg 168)
1. Mick Harford
2. Glenn Roeder
3. Peter Beardsley
4. Imre Varadi
5. Terry McDermott
6. Martin Thomas
7. John Anderson
8. David McCreery
9. Mick Channon
10. Jeff Clarke
11. Malcolm Brown

The Boys of '76 (pg 170)
1. Chicago Sting
2. Middlesbrough
3. Liverpool
4. Blackburn Rovers
5. Arsenal
6. Birmingham City
7. Burnley
8. Aston Villa
9. Cardiff City
10. Arsenal
11. Bolton Wanderers
12. Washington Diplomats

Bright Sparks (pg 172)

1. Fulham, Huddersfield Town
2. Carlisle United, Heart of Midlothian, Plymouth Argyle, Hartlepool United
3. Stockport County
4. Bury, Charlton Athletic, Rochdale, Carlisle United, Blackpool, Sunderland
5. Stoke City
6. Leyton Orient, Nottingham Forest, Manchester City
7. Fulham, Halifax Town
8. Norwich City, Blackpool, Stockport County, Stoke City, West Bromwich, Nottingham Forest, Leicester City, Bolton Wanderers, Sheffield Wednesday
9. Bradford Park Avenue, Cardiff City, Newport County
10. Burnley
11. Sunderland, Carlisle United
12. Peterborough United, Barnsley, Blackburn Rovers, Bury

The Rucks (pg 174)

1. Lee Bowyer and Kieron Dyer
2. David Batty
3. Joey Barton
4. Fabricio Coloccini and Mike Williamson
5. Duncan Ferguson
6. Billy Bremner
7. Kevin Muscat   8. Roy Keane
9. Massadio Haïdara
10. Duncan Ferguson
11. Joey Barton

Marching On Together (pg 176)

1. Jonathan Woodgate
2. Gary Speed
3. Mark Viduka   4. Alan Smith
5. Vurnon Anita   6. David Batty
7. Ian Rush

Meet the New Boss, Same as the Old Boss (pg 178)

1. Manchester City
2. Chelsea   3. Norwich City
4. Blackburn Rovers
5. West Ham United and Bolton Wanderers
6. Liverpool
7. Brighton & Hove Albion
8. Fulham   9. Crystal Palace
10. Liverpool   11. Burnley
12. Norwich City

Fall Out Boys (pg 180)

1. Willie Donachie   2. Joe Kinnear
3. Alan Pardew   4. Graeme Souness
5. John Carver   6. Dennis Wise

Bad Boys, Bad Boys (pg 182)

1. Alan Pardew   2. Duncan Ferguson
3. Andy Carroll   4. Joey Barton
5. Nile Ranger   6. Billy Whitehurst
7. Rolando Aarons   8. Lee Bowyer and Jonathan Woodgate

Tooners & Gooners (pg 184)

1. Kenny Sansom
2. George Eastham
3. Sol Campbell
4. Andy Cole   5. Joe Willock
6. Mathieu Debuchy
7. Pat Howard

To Victor Go The Spoils (pg 186)

1. Akinwunmi   2. Malachi
3. Courtney   4. Mathieson
5. Roland   6. Andrew
7. Piaras   8. Irénée   9. Edwin
10. Grattan   11. Albino   12. Ian
13. Douglas   14. Patrick

Many Happy Returns (pg 188)

1. Peter Beardsley
2. Pavel Srníček
3. Nolberto Solano
4. Mark McGhee   5. Rob Elliott
6. Terry Hibbitt   7. Andy Carroll
8. John Craggs   9. David Mills
10. Tommy Wright   11. Lee Clark

Player of the Year (pg 190)

1. Nolberto Solano
2. Olivier Bernard   3. Habib Beye
4. Sébastien Bassong
5. José Enrique
6. Fabricio Coloccini
7. Tim Krul   8. Davide Santon
9. Daryl Janmaat
10. Salomón Rondón
11. Martin Dúbravka

Gullit's Gambles (pg 192)

1. Duncan Ferguson   2. Kieron Dyer
3. Alain Goma   4. Marcelino
5. Silvio Marić   6. Didier Domi

Big Sam's Shopping (pg 194)

1. Alan Smith
2. José Enrique   3. Joey Barton
4. David Rozehnal   5. Habib Bèye
6. Abdoulaye Fayé   7. Tamás Kádár
8. Ben Tozer   9. Geremi

Kenny's Captures (pg 196)

1. Gary Speed
2. Alessandro Pistone
3. Andreas Andersson
4. Jon Dahl Tomasson
5. Des Hamilton
6. Andy Griffin
7. Nikolaos Dabizas
8. Georgios Georgiadis
9. Brian Pinas
10. Temur Ketsbaia
11. John Barnes
12. Stuart Pearce   13. Ian Rush
14. Dietmar Hamann

Going Dutch (pg 198)

1. Jetro Willems
2. Patrick van Aanholt
3. John Karelse
4. Daryl Janmaat   5. Tim Krul
6. Patrick Kluivert
7. Georginio Wijnaldum

The Ever-Presents (pg 200)

1. Jimmy Lawrence
2. Frank Hudspeth
3. Shay Given   4. Frank Clark

Celeb Supporters (pg 202)

1. Cheryl Cole
2. Brian Blessed   3. Gabby Logan
4. Ant and Dec   5. Brian Johnson
6. Jimmy Nail   7. Bryan Ferry
8. Robson Green   9. James Bay
10. John McCririck

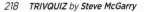

TRIVQUIZ

FROM ABBA TO ZAPPA, AMÉLIE TO ZULU, AND AGÜERO TO ZIDANE

NEW FOOTBALL AND POP CULTURE QUIZZES
EVERY DAY AT TRIVQUIZ.COM

 trivquiz.com   trivquiz   trivquiz   trivquizcomic